ALL ABOUT SEASONS

Written by Jo Graham

NURSERY WORLD
TES
THE TIMES EDUCATIONAL SUPPLEMENT

NURSERY WORLD

TES
THE TIMES EDUCATIONAL SUPPLEMENT

Managing Editor Patricia Grogan
Art Editor Clare Shedden

Photography Andy Crawford

Assistant Editor Edward FitzGerald
Consultant Marian Whitehead

First published in Great Britain in 1999 by
Times Supplements Limited
Admiral House, 66–68 East Smithfield, London E1 9XY

A CIP catalogue record for this book is available from the British Library

ISBN 1-84122-009-4

Colour reproduction by Prima Creatives Services, UK
Printed and bound in Belgium by Proost

Nursery World would like to thank the children and staff at the following Bringing Up Baby nurseries for taking part in this book:
Richford Gate Nursery, London,
Brondesbury Park Nursery, London

CONTENTS

INTRODUCTION

All About Seasons contains more than 100 activities divided into six chapters. Each chapter explores one avenue of the book's central theme. The activities are self-contained but also build from each other, so you can either dip into several chapters when planning your theme or you can use complete chapters. All the activities are firmly underpinned by seven areas of learning to help you incorporate them into your planning. The topic web on pages 10–11 shows you into which areas of learning each activity falls and each activity has symbols representing the areas of learning covered.

Planning a curriculum

The activites in this book are suitable for curriculum planning following all the early-years guidelines across the United Kingdom. It is widely accepted that young children learn most effectively through first-hand experiences presented through investigative, sensory, imaginative, creative and constructive, play-based activities. Children should be given opportunities to observe, represent, recall, describe, and question. This book gives many ideas for developing these skills, although it should not be seen as providing a complete curriculum. The book's main purpose is to help you build a balanced, varied and interesting curriculum for children of nursery age when presenting aspects of the complex theme of Seasons. Each activity covers one or more of the following areas of learning: Personal, Social and Emotional Development, Language and Literacy, Mathematics, Science and Technology, Time and Place, Physical Development, Creative Development.

Personal, Social and Emotional Development

This area of development is crucial in the early years setting. It is all about children being and belonging, developing confidence and taking control over their thoughts and actions and understanding what it is to function outside of the family.

Children are developing from parallel players to co-operators. They are building friendships and trying out different behaviours. They will need to test and reflect with adults on the rules of being in nursery and to discuss their feelings. Children will be developing as decision makers and independent thinkers and these skills should be developed throughout their learning. From cooking activities to art work, children should be encouraged to do as much of the activity as they can for themselves with strategic adult intervention to avoid danger or frustration.

It is vital at this early stage of developing a sense of self that children learn to value other people's differences, be they cultural, religious, racial, gender or disability based. It is equally vital that the experiences they have give value to their own distinct personalities and backgrounds.

Language and Literacy

Talking and listening are a vital first component of children's language acquisition. Encourage children to talk to you, to other children, to their parents and carers about everything they are doing. Look to develop a wide range of talking including: reporting events in their lives, describing what they can sense or feel, making up stories or re-telling old favourites, reciting rhymes or poems, singing songs, asking their own questions and responding to adult-led talk.

A home corner is not stimulating enough to be the only role-play opportunity on offer. Try adding new props, stimulating the play with stories or an event. Additionally, try packing the house away for a while and replacing it with a shop, a café, a library or a hospital.

Research has shown that children who develop a sense of themselves as language users develop their language skills to a greater extent. Young children need to come into contact with a wide range of language forms and try using them themselves. Every attempt has value.

In writing, early mark making is crucial to children recognising both the purpose and form of our written languages. In reading, children should delight in books. Young children become adept at decoding pictures so, when choosing books for children to look at by themselves, always go for well illustrated ones. Include fiction, information, poetry and rhyme books.

Although there is value in reading favourite books over and over, try to vary the books on offer. Look for alternative versions of the same stories, borrow library books to supplement your own and encourage children to share their favourite books from home.

Mathematics

For future success in mathematics pre-school children need to develop a strong sense of number and a feel for shape and space. Young children need to understand that numbers only ever represent other things. Whilst learning their numbers is important, it is more important to count things, to match and sort, to look at sets and estimate how many things there might be there, to recognise patterns (for example the spots on a dice) and to play with taking number sets apart and putting them back together.

Sorting, matching and counting opportunities arise throughout the rest of the curriculum from serving customers in the pretend shop or café to working out how many beads you need for your latest jewellery creation. The maths in this book builds on these opportunities.

Equally, using comparative language, shape vocabulary or positional language can all come through story, role-play, construction and craft activities. The key is to ensure that any adults helping children with these activities are alive to the mathematical learning you have planned and focus the children in a way that prompts them to include these aspects in their play.

Singing number songs and rhymes can help children towards the idea of putting numbers together and taking them away. Other things to try include number lines and number line games, board games and sharing out resources.

All children are different and will have different abilities and needs. Some children at four years can handle numbers to 100 whilst others are still learning to count to 10. To avoid more able children becoming frustrated remember to plan some activities that allow children to play with numbers bigger than 10.

Science and Technology

Pre-school science should mainly be about encouraging a sense of wonder and curiosity in children. Children should want to ask questions such as 'what will happen if..?' and 'why does that happen..?' and know how to

safely go about finding out the answers.

There are opportunities for raising these kinds of questions in many activities not traditionally seen as science. Art and technology, particularly cooking, are especially good areas.

The main science ideas about the seasons which children will be working towards are:

- that the weather changes according to the seasons
- that the amount of daylight changes
- that the natural world responds to these changes
- that the seasons come in regular order

As they get older they will learn that the seasons are the result of where we are on the globe. As the Earth spins on its axis, it is at a slight angle. Hence as it orbits the Sun (in one year) parts of the Earth are closer or further away from it.

Technology is an umbrella term covering model making and using technological equipment. Technology gives children the chance to develop making skills. At this stage children cannot be expected to plan in great detail, but they should be encouraged to reflect on their finished model and think what worked and what didn't. Children should be encouraged to choose and explore both tools and materials and to try out different ways of making and joining things. They may need help to master new tools safely but should be given a wide range of tools to try.

Time and Place

Alongside developing a sense of self, children are developing a sense of time and place. They are examining where and with whom they belong. They avidly construct family histories and relationships, often trying to place themselves at past events. Activities in this book build on the skill of remembering and of developing this sense of things changing over time.

Children develop their sense of place through first-hand experience. It is important to start with what children already know and so activities in this book emphasise taking children out into the locality, re-visiting the same features throughout the year to see how they have changed and looking at what lives and grows near our homes. Activities in this book also move children towards an awareness that there are many other places around the world, most of which are very different from our place. Understanding the seasons is

inextricably linked with seeing the Earth in relationship to the Sun, so many of the activities are aimed at starting children towards an understanding of our place being Earth.

Physical Development

This area of development covers both gross and fine motor skills and physical well-being. Young children need to build confidence and control through activities such as running, jumping, stretching, balancing, dancing and so on. At the same time they need to develop the fine movements and control needed for small scale work such as threading, cutting, model building, drawing, sticking and eventually writing.

Pre-school children are very physical, often using physical activity as a way of exploring their world as much as they do to build their muscles or master movement. Pre-school planning should encompass physical activity and movement as an integral part of the day.

Creative Development

In this area of learning, young children express their feelings, responses and observations through a wide range of different media.

The art area should offer a huge variety of different materials to explore for both 2- and 3-D work and children should be encouraged to experiment with different tools and resources as well as choose them for specific tasks. Fabrics, collage materials, a range of papers, thick and thin paint brushes, other tools for applying paint such as sponges, combs, rollers and so on, readymix paint, powder paint, poster paint, a range of glues, wax crayons, oil pastels, felt tipped pens, pencil crayons, chalks and charcoal should all be available. Clay, play dough, re-usable materials and construction kits should give children opportunities to model in 3-D.

Young children should also be given frequent opportunities to express themselves in music and dance. This book suggests ideas for creating musical pieces, but children also need to listen to a wide variety of music from different cultures and traditions, to dance freely and to experiment with sounds from all sorts of instruments. As well as the percussive instruments common in nurseries, try to give children opportunities to strum guitars or blow woodwind instruments. Invite parents who can play instruments to perform for you as children need to see that practice can lead to mastery.

Planning your theme

Not every theme you plan can cover every aspect important to children's learning. What is crucial is that, over time, the curriculum is broad and balanced. Whilst each theme may have a distinctive flavour, most allow you to plan learning outcomes in the main curriculum areas. Imaginative play is also good for offering learning opportunities across all subjects.

Planning a theme

When planning a new theme, look for ways to extend things you always have on offer in your early-years setting. Could the sand become a desert or the moon? Can the house corner change into a hospital? What new materials can you add to the art corner? Are there different stories, poetry or information books you could add to the reading area? Are there CD ROMs or websites that children could explore that link to your theme?

Taking children out of the setting and inviting visitors in in connection with your theme is an excellent way of building children's special skills and feeding their curiosity about how the outside world works. Large scale visits to museums and farms can be rewarding, but a walk to the local shops or a bus ride can be equally inspirational for young children.

New themes offer new possibilities for linking with children's homes. Effective learning is based on what children already know, so links to children's home life is vital. Do any parents or grandparents have interests, hobbies, skills or jobs that connect to your theme? Does your theme offer possible activities that would be straightforward for adults to help with in nursery? Are there activities that could involve bringing in things or information from home? Are there chances to learn about different cultures or traditions and if so are there

family adults or community leaders who would be willing to help out?

Planning learning is a high level skill. Whilst planning ahead is crucial to allow you to organise visitors to nursery and to marshal resources, it can be restrictive and not allow for spontaneity. Capitalising on children's own interests and unforeseen occurrences can be highly motivating for young children. A digger arriving outside nursery one day to fix a burst water pipe should not be ignored, but the excitement caused should be harnessed as far as possible and incorporated into the day's learning.

Teaching Poetry

Whilst young children are likely to be familiar with nursery rhymes, they may not have much experience of poetry. It is important to expose children to as wide a range of poetry styles as possible. Poems for children do not always have to rhyme. Children are as interested in the rhythm or sound of words as they are in rhymes.

Reading different types of poetry to children is a good start, but remember to also include poetry books in displays and book shelves and to feature poetry cassette tapes in listening corners.

Some adults are sceptical of young children's ability to create their own poetry. Making up poems, however, is a valuable language tool for young children. Poems can create an effect with far fewer words than a story and can be more expressive of feelings. We should not expect adult-style poetry from nursery children in exactly the same way that we do not expect complex stories or master standard art works. Children's poems may well not conform to a particular style and will almost certainly not rhyme. This is not important. What is crucial is that children understand poetry as a form and make first efforts to create their own.

One way to introduce poetry is to look at rhymes inside birthday cards. Give each child a card and ask them to make up what the rhyme inside might say. Another starting point is to play with rhymes and songs children already know, making up new verses or supplying new endings.

Once children feel confident to suggest their own ideas they can either dictate their poems to an adult to scribe or record them on to a cassette tape. Alternatively children may work better in a group writing a poem together. With an adult facilitating, children can offer their ideas, words and phrases and as a group decide which order these should go in to create the final piece. Adults can help the feel of the poem by suggesting elements of structure such as repeating the first line of the poem at the end to round it off.

This book suggests a number of poetry ideas, including making up versions of well-known songs and creating your own poems. These activities should always be founded on a basis of familiarity with poems from a variety of cultures and traditions.

How to use this book

All About Seasons is divided into six self-contained chapters that develop one avenue of the book's central theme. Each chapter has its own coloured bands to help you identify which chapter you are in and its own contents list. The contents list gives you a summary of each activity to help you decide which activities to use. The materials needed for each activity are always found at the top left of the actvity and the educational aims are underneath.

Educational symbols

Each activity introduces one or more areas of learning. The symbols show you which areas are covered and the accompanying text gives you the specific aims.

This symbol shows the activity will develop aspects of language and literacy

This symbol shows the activity will develop aspects of science and technology

This symbol shows the activity will develop aspects of creative development

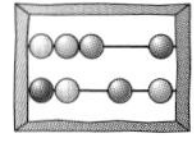
This symbol shows the activity will develop aspects of mathematics

This symbol shows the activity will develop aspects of personal, social and emotional development

This symbol shows the activity will develop aspects of physical development

This symbol shows the activity will develop aspects of time and place

Each activity is numbered for easy reference.

The triangle and circle show you the suggested adult-child ratio for the activity.

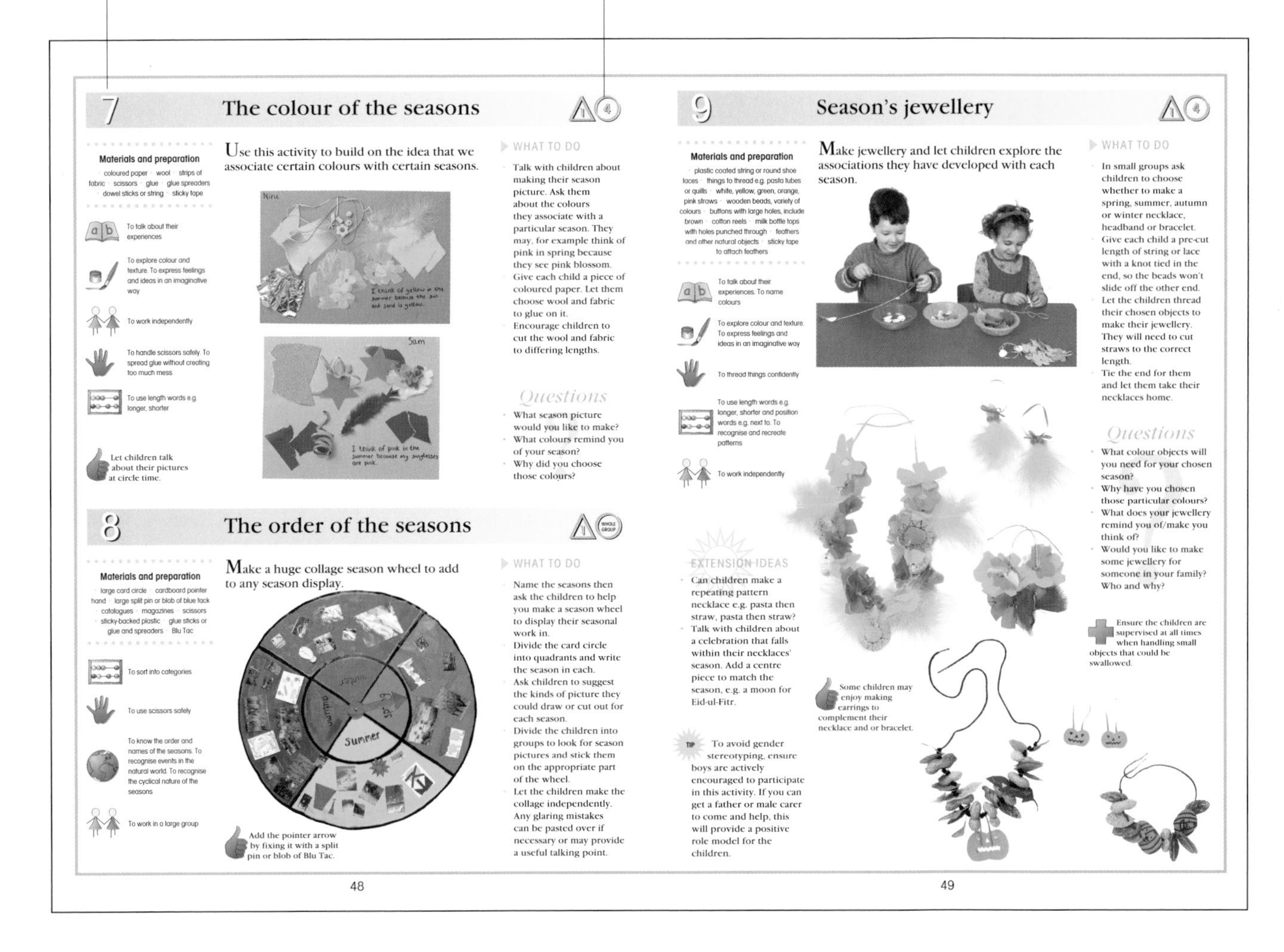

7 The colour of the seasons

Materials and preparation
coloured paper · wool · strips of fabric · scissors · glue · glue spreaders · dowel sticks or string · sticky tape

To talk about their experiences

To explore colour and texture. To express feelings and ideas in an imaginative way

To work independently

To handle scissors safely. To spread glue without creating too much mess

To use length words e.g. longer, shorter

Let children talk about their pictures at circle time.

Use this activity to build on the idea that we associate certain colours with certain seasons.

Nira
I think of yellow in the summer because the sun and sand is yellow.
Sam
I think of pink in the summer because my sunglasses are pink.

WHAT TO DO

- Talk with children about making their season picture. Ask them about the colours they associate with a particular season. They may, for example think of pink in spring because they see pink blossom.
- Give each child a piece of coloured paper. Let them choose wool and fabric to glue on it.
- Encourage children to cut the wool and fabric to differing lengths.

Questions

- What season picture would you like to make?
- What colours remind you of your season?
- Why did you choose those colours?

8 The order of the seasons

Materials and preparation
large card circle · cardboard pointer hand · large split pin or blob of blue tack · catalogues · magazines · scissors · sticky-backed plastic · glue sticks or glue and spreaders · Blu Tac

To sort into categories

To use scissors safely

To know the order and names of the seasons. To recognise events in the natural world. To recognise the cyclical nature of the seasons

To work in a large group

Make a huge collage season wheel to add to any season display.

winter
autumn
spring
Summer

Add the pointer arrow by fixing it with a split pin or blob of Blu Tac.

WHAT TO DO

- Name the seasons then ask the children to help you make a season wheel to display their seasonal work in.
- Divide the card circle into quadrants and write the season in each.
- Ask children to suggest the kinds of picture they could draw or cut out for each season.
- Divide the children into groups to look for season pictures and stick them on the appropriate part of the wheel.
- Let the children make the collage independently. Any glaring mistakes can be pasted over if necessary or may provide a useful talking point.

48

9 Season's jewellery

Materials and preparation
plastic coated string or round shoe laces · things to thread e.g. pasta tubes or quills · white, yellow, green, orange, pink straws · wooden beads, variety of colours · buttons with large holes, include brown · cotton reels · milk bottle tops with holes punched through · feathers and other natural objects · sticky tape to attach feathers

To talk about their experiences. To name colours

To explore colour and texture. To express feelings and ideas in an imaginative way

To thread things confidently

To use length words e.g. longer, shorter and position words e.g. next to. To recognise and recreate patterns

To work independently

Make jewellery and let children explore the associations they have developed with each season.

WHAT TO DO

- In small groups ask children to choose whether to make a spring, summer, autumn or winter necklace, headband or bracelet.
- Give each child a pre-cut length of string or lace with a knot tied in the end, so the beads won't slide off the other end.
- Let the children thread their chosen objects to make their jewellery. They will need to cut straws to the correct length.
- Tie the end for them and let them take their necklaces home.

Questions

- What colour objects will you need for your chosen season?
- Why have you chosen those particular colours?
- What does your jewellery remind you of/make you think of?
- Would you like to make some jewellery for someone in your family? Who and why?

EXTENSION IDEAS

- Can children make a repeating pattern necklace e.g. pasta then straw, pasta then straw?
- Talk with children about a celebration that falls within their necklaces' season. Add a centre piece to match the season, e.g. a moon for Eid-ul-Fitr.

Some children may enjoy making earrings to complement their necklace and or bracelet.

Ensure the children are supervised at all times when handling small objects that could be swallowed.

TIP To avoid gender stereotyping, ensure boys are actively encouraged to participate in this activity. If you can get a father or male carer to come and help, this will provide a positive role model for the children.

49

Additional symbols

Many activities have additional hints and tips or safety points. They are identified by the symbols shown below.

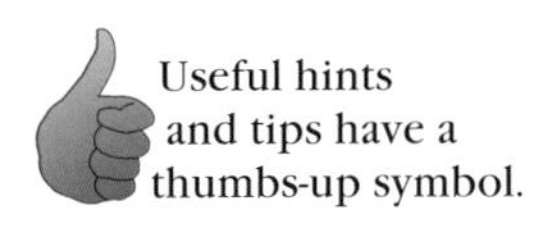
Useful hints and tips have a thumbs-up symbol.

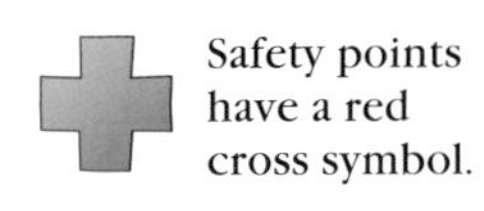
Safety points have a red cross symbol.

Breaking down the information

Each activity either has step-by-step instructions or bullet-pointed instructions under the heading 'What To Do'. Many activities also have suggested questions and extension ideas, also under the appropriate headings.

One or more helpful suggestions for increasing an activity's learning value have a star symbol.

Topic web

Each activity in this book is underpinned by one or more areas of learning. This topic web lists all the activities that develop each area of learning under the appropriate heading. Use this web when planning your curriculum to ensure that the activities you organise develop all areas of learning according to the particular early years guidelines you are following. The activities will help you create an educationally exciting and balanced theme that your children will love!

CREATIVE DEVELOPMENT

- What is spring? (1) page 13
- How the wind blows (3) page 14
- Paper bag kites (4) page 14
- Blossoming trees (5) page 15
- Flowers in bloom (6) page 15
- Growing up (8) page 16
- Cuddly animals (12) page 18
- I like spring (13) page 19
- Spring dance (14) page 19
- Summer trees (7) page 24
- Seaside role play (11) page 26
- Hibernating animals (3) page 30
- Autumn secrets (4) page 30
- The colour of autumn (6) page 31
- Autumn sound effects (14) page 35
- Salty snow (7) page 40
- Winter trees (9) page 41
- Chinese New Year (14) page 43
- The colour of the seasons (7) page 48
- Season's jewellery (9) page 49
- Off on holiday (15) page 52
- Four seasons face painting (17) page 53
- Snowdrops and crocuses (2) page 55
- Growing movements (4) page 56
- Musical change (9) page 59

LANGUAGE AND LITERACY

- What kind of weather? (2) page 13
- How the wind blows (3) page 14
- Flowers in bloom (6) page 15
- Visiting a farm (9) page 17
- Visiting a pond (10) page 17
- Who's my mother? (11) page 18
- I like spring (13) page 19
- What is summer? (1) page 21
- Summer begins with S (2) page 21
- Sunny summer morning (3) page 22
- Eating outside (9) page 25
- Cooking outside (10) page 25
- Seaside role play (11) page 26
- Summer sports (12) page 27
- What happens in autumn? (1) page 29
- Hibernating animals (3) page 30
- Sleeping trees (5) page 31
- The colour of autumn (6) page 31
- Playing at greengrocers (8) page 32
- Autumn festivals (9) page 33
- Rainy autumn days (11) page 34
- Keeping dry (12) page 34
- Autumn poem (13) page 35
- What happens in winter? (1) page 37
- Dressing up warm (2) page 37
- Hats and more hats (3) page 38
- The North wind blows (5) page 39
- The snowman (6) page 39
- Salty snow (7) page 40
- What is snow made of? (8) page 40
- Winter trees (9) page 41
- Evergreens (10) page 41
- Your favourite weather (1) page 45
- A year in the park (3) page 46
- A tree for all seasons (5) page 47
- The colour of the seasons (7) page 48
- Season's jewellery (9) page 49
- All the special times (12) page 51
- Weather round the world (14) page 52
- Off on holiday (15) page 52
- Four seasons face painting (17) page 53
- Looking for signs of change (1) page 55
- Roots and shoots (3) page 56
- Days are changing (5) page 57
- How do you feel today? (6) page 57
- How have you changed? (8) page 58
- Musical change (9) page 59

TIME AND PLACE

- What kind of weather? (2) page 13
- Paper bag kites (4) page 14
- Looking at seeds (7) page 16
- Visiting a farm (9) page 17
- Sunny summer morning (3) page 22
- Changing shadows (5) page 23
- Summer trees (7) page 24
- Beautiful butterflies (8) page 24
- Eating outside (9) page 25
- What happens in autumn?(1) page 29
- Autumn secrets (4) page 30
- Sleeping trees (5) page 31
- Keeping dry (12) page 34
- The Snowman (6) page 39
- What is snow made of? (8) page 40
- A year in the park (3) page 46
- A tree for all seasons (5) page 47
- The seasons game (6) page 47
- The order of the seasons (8) page 48
- Which season? (10) page 50
- Year round mobile (11) page 50
- All the special times (12) page 51
- Weather round the world (14) page 52
- Off on holiday (15) page 52
- How have you changed? (8) page 58

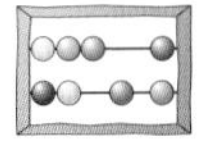

Mathematics

Physical development

Science and technology

Personal social and emotional development

SPRING

This chapter looks at spring, focusing on birth and new life, the awakening of life after the cold winter and looking forward to the bright summer. The activities give children lots of opportunities to explore colours and textures associated with nature in the spring. Many of the activities involve going outside with the children. Spring is a good time to take children out of the early-years setting, helping them to observe their environment and developing a sense of wonder at the changes that the increasing light and warmer weather bring about. Remember to ensure you have high adult–child ratios for these activities to ensure maximum learning potential in a safe environment.

Activities in this chapter

1 What is spring?

Materials and preparation

- objects to lead the discussion into growing things, the weather or other aspects of spring such as crocuses, wellington boots, trowel, seeds, umbrella
- range of art materials
- range of posters, pictures and books

To work as part of a group. To initiate ideas and solve problems

To use a wide range of resources to communicate feelings

To recognise features of events in the natural world

Questions

- What do you know about the spring?
- What will spring weather be like?
- What do you think comes after spring?

Make a spring display with children and encourage them to express their feelings about the spring.

TIPS

- If you have two groups, either make a display large enough for both to share or give each group a separate display. Talk about what each group has chosen with the other.
- Older children might want to add labels to the display.

WHAT TO DO

- We often make displays to stimulate discussions. Try starting with the discussion and let children make the display.
- Remind them how dark and cold it was in winter. Ask how the changing weather and longer days make them feel.
- Let the children choose the backdrop for the display and which pictures or items to add to it. Ask what they could bring in from home and how they might arrange the displays.

2 What kind of weather?

Materials and preparation

- calendar or grid to form weather chart
- recording of television weather forecast

To develop an understanding of yesterday, today, tomorrow. To name different types of weather

To listen and responds to rhymes and sayings

TIPS

- Ask parents and grandparents for other weather sayings.
- At the end of March and April remind children of the sayings. Ask, have they come true?

Use these spring weather sayings to talk with children about weather forecasting and to reinforce their awareness of yesterday, today and tomorrow.

March winds and April showers bring forth May flowers

March comes in like a lion, goes out like a lamb

WHAT TO DO

- Use circle time to recite the two sayings. Point out March and April on your calendar.
- Ask how many children have seen the weather forecast on television. Explain that sayings like these were used before television, so people could predict the weather.
- In small groups, ask the children to describe today's weather, then yesterday's. Scribe their comments on a simple grid. Now ask the children to predict tomorrow's weather and add these to the grid.
- Remind children the next day to check their predictions.

3 How the wind blows

Materials and preparation

• light things such as: chiffon, silk or cotton scarves, plastic carrier bags or balloons on strings • 'Mrs Mopple's Washing line' (see resources)

To talk about their experiences

To develop an awareness of space

To respond imaginatively to what they feel

Introduce this activity by reading 'Mrs Mopple's Washing Line' to the children.

Extend the activity by reading 'The wind blew' (see resources).

WHAT TO DO

- March is often very windy. Take the opportunity to raise children's awareness of the wind pushing them and point out that the wind has direction.
- Go outside on a windy day. Let children pretend they are leaves or feathers being blown by the wind.
- Ask children to say which way the wind is blowing them.
- Let them hold up light things. Can they see which way the wind is blowing?

4 Paper bag kites

Materials and preparation

• paper bags • collage materials • felt-tipped pens • string • 'Mrs Mopple's Washing line' (see resources)

To explore features of the natural world

To explore texture, colour and shape

To handle tools and materials safely

Reinforce children's awareness of wind direction by making kites.

1 Lay out the materials. Ask the children to decorate one bag each with spring pictures.

2 Make holes either side of the open end of the bag and thread string through to form a handle.

3 Secure the ends with knots or sticky tape. Let children fly their kites. Read 'Mrs Mopple's Washing Line' and talk to children about what might happen to their kites if the wind blows too strongly.

Only fly kites in wide open spaces.

The paper bag kites will stand up to a moderate breeze but not very strong winds.

WHAT TO DO

- There are many ways to make kites. Below we give instructions using cardboard tubes and on the left we give instructions using paper bags.
- Make streamers to show wind direction. Decorate cardboard tubes and fix long strips of paper to one end. Fix a string loop to the other end and tie securely outside a window. Watch which way the streamers flutter.

Questions

- What makes your kite fly?
- When does it fly best?
- Which way should you hold your kite: into the wind or against it?

5 Blossoming trees

Materials and preparation

- branches (real or home-made from rolled newspaper, painted brown)
- flower pot
- stones
- collage materials: e.g. range of fabrics, tissue paper, cotton wool, wool, toilet tissue
- string or sticky tape

To select materials and equipment. To recognise features of living things

To respond to what they see, feel and smell

Visit a local tree to start children thinking about spring as the start of new life.

Questions

- Is your blossom just one colour?
- Is it a dark or light colour?
- What other colours can you see on your blossom?

WHAT TO DO

- Visit a tree locally that is beginning to blossom. Talk about the colour, smell and feel of the blossom.
- Name the parts of the tree and take rubbings.
- Back at the nursery stand fallen branches (or home-made ones) in a large pot weighted down with stones.
- Ask children to choose collage materials of the right colour to stick on the branches as blossom.
- Choose matching wool or cotton thread to wrap round the 'blossom' or use sticky tape.

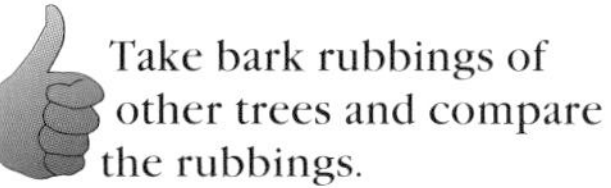

Take bark rubbings of other trees and compare the rubbings.

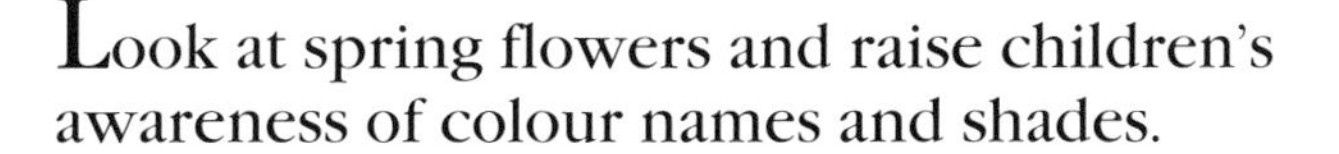

6 Flowers in bloom

Materials and preparation

- spring flowers in a variety of colours and shades, e.g. crocuses, daffodils, jonquils, narcissi, forsythia
- range of powder paints
- mixing pallettes
- sugar paper
- paint brushes in a range of thicknesses

To name flowers and flower parts

To explore colour and shape

To know colour names and lighter/darker

Look at spring flowers and raise children's awareness of colour names and shades.

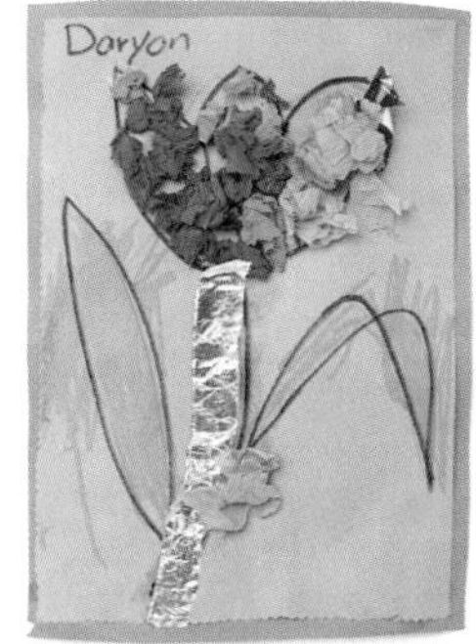

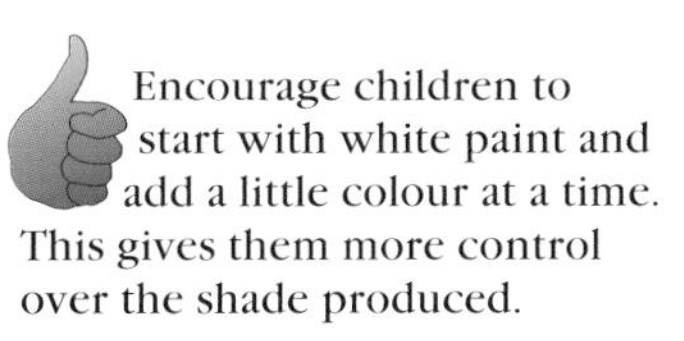

Encourage children to start with white paint and add a little colour at a time. This gives them more control over the shade produced.

EXTENSION IDEA

- Keep the painted shapes as spring colours to compare with other seasons and to make a Colours Around the Year display.

WHAT TO DO

- Look at some spring flowers. Talk with the children about each one. Name the flowers but focusing particularly on their colour.
- Ask the children to compare two flowers of similar colour, e.g. daffodil and narcissus.
- Let each small group choose two flowers. Give each group just their colour and white paint. Can they mix the right shade to match their flowers? Younger children may need help mixing different shades.
- Paint pictures of the flowers with the specially mixed paint or simply paint paper plates and add green garden canes for stalks.

7 Looking at seeds

Materials and preparation

- range of seeds
- 1 plant pot for 2 children
- potting compost
- dwarf sunflower seeds
- pencils to aid planting seeds
- watering cans

To care for living things and develop a sense of time by looking at growth

To work purposefully alongside another child

To make observations and keep records

TIP Harvest the sunflower seeds in autumn and save to plant next spring.

Reinforce the theme of new growth in spring by growing sunflowers with the children.

1 Ask each pair to fill their pot with compost and bury five seeds in the soil.

2 Water the seeds regularly. Once small shoots have grown, pull out all but the strongest one.

3 Continue to water the shoot and watch it grow into a large sunflower. Keep a record of its growth.

WHAT TO DO

- Look at a range of seeds and talk with chidren about what they look like: their shape, colour, size and pattern.
- Grow dwarf sunflowers with the children – full size sunflowers may become unmanageable as they take up a lot of space.
- Keep a daily record of the changes and discuss them with the children.
- Introduce appropriate language such as petals, flower, stem, shoots.

Questions

- How are the sunflower seeds different to the other seeds?
- What do you think will happen to the seeds when we plant them?
- What will we need to do to look after our seeds?

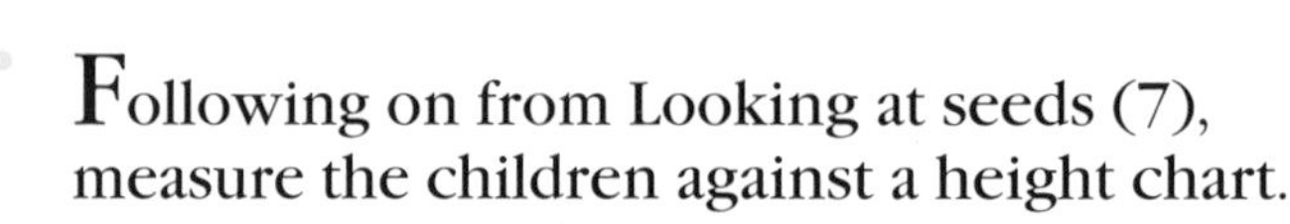

8 Growing up

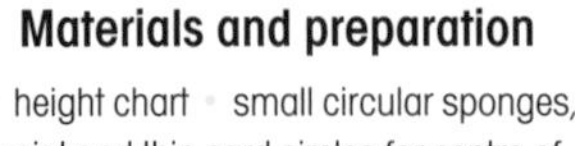

Materials and preparation

- height chart
- small circular sponges, paint and thin card circles for centre of flower
- yellow play paper for petals
- thick green card for sunflower stems
- brown paint for printing
- scissors
- stapler or split pins (always supervise use)
- paper clips
- sticky tape
- glue

To work creatively with a range of art materials

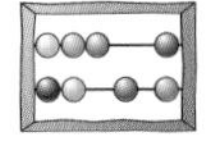

To use comparative size language: bigger, taller, shorter, same

Questions

- Are the sunflowers all the same height?
- Why do you think some have grown more than others?

Following on from Looking at seeds (7), measure the children against a height chart. Discuss who is taller and shorter than who.

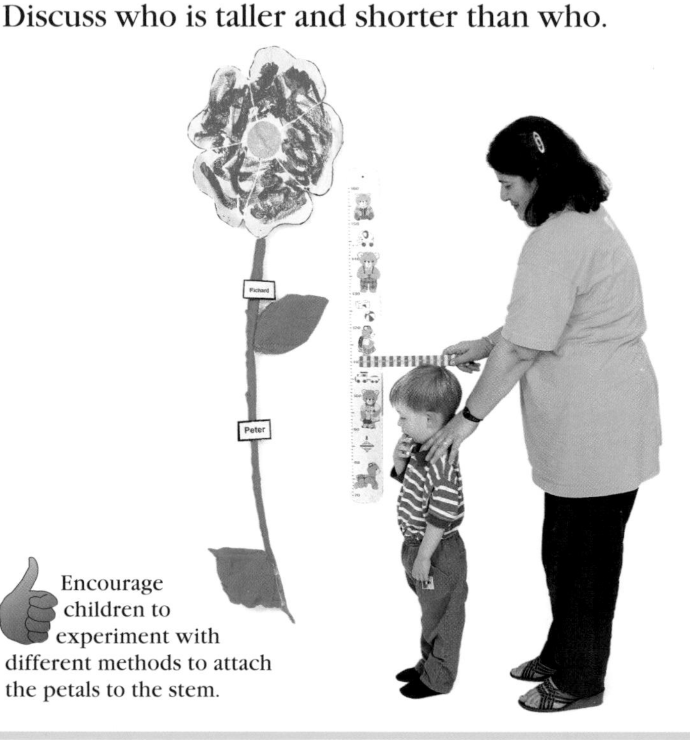

Encourage children to experiment with different methods to attach the petals to the stem.

WHAT TO DO

- When the sunflowers planted above are two handspans high, ask children to make sunflowers the same height.
- Give each child a strip of green card to measure against the stem of their flower. Help them make a mark at the correct height.
- Let children cut their stem and then cut out petals from play paper.
- Sponge print card circles for the centre of their flower and let them fix petals around the edge.
- Ask the children to use their sunflowers as measuring sticks around the setting.

9 Visiting a farm

To recognise animals and their babies

To listen attentively and talk about experiences

TIPS Ensure you have a high adult-child ratio and all adults understand the purpose of the visit and their specific roles.
- Send a permission letter home before the trip. Explain the nature of the visit, its purpose and what the children need to bring - include wet weather clothes and sun protection.

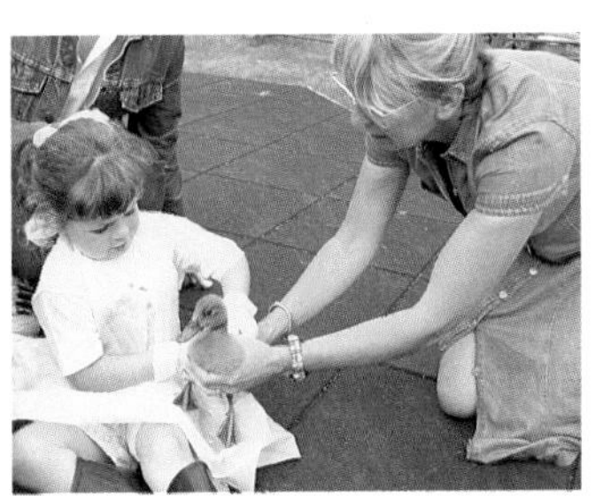

Use a visit to a farm to show children that many animals have babies in the spring.

Ensure you know where the hand-washing facilities are and that children wash their hands after handling animals and before eating.

WHAT TO DO

- Visit the farm before the trip and check when you can see the baby animals. Make a note of facilities - eating areas, toilets, shelter etc.
- Make a mental timetable, thinking when each facility will be needed during the trip.
- Think about what else children can learn.
- Take photographs around the farm to stimulate planning discussions with children.
- Plan all aspects of the visit with the children and other adults.

Questions

- What baby animals shall we look for at the farm?
- What else might we see?
- What shall we try to find out when at the farm?
- What shall we photograph?

10 Visiting a pond

Materials and preparation

- range of picture books showing pondlife, such as 'In the small, small pond' and 'See how they grow' series (see resources)

To care for living things

To recognise animals and their babies

To listen attentively and talk about experiences

If you collect any wildlife at the pond to study back at nursery, keep it in a habitat close to its natural one and return it to the pond within two days.

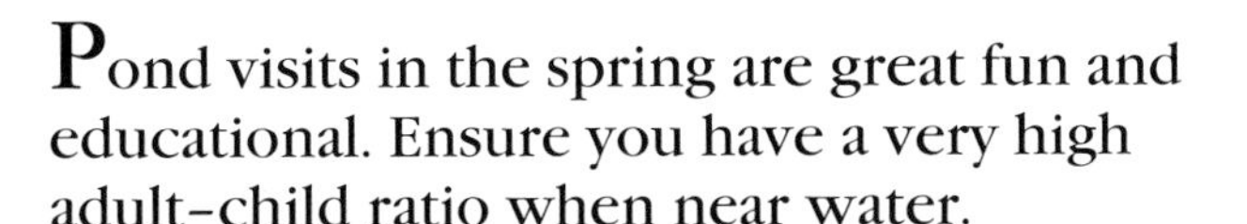

Pond visits in the spring are great fun and educational. Ensure you have a very high adult-child ratio when near water.

TIP Take as many adult helpers with you as possible. Make sure they know what the focus of your visit is so that they can help children to get the most from it.
- As with the farm visit, send a permission/information letter home.

WHAT TO DO

- Visit the pond on your own first to ensure it is safe for small children. Fenced ponds are best for very small children.
- Before the visit talk about the kinds of thing that live in or near ponds. Look at picture books, lifecycle puzzles and models of the animals.

11 Who's my mother?

Materials and preparation

toy farm animals · tray · cloth · 'Where is my baby?' 'I am a ...' series, 'See how they grow' series (see resources)

To respond to stories and join in role play

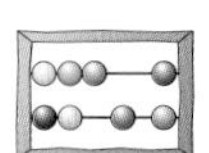

To match mother to young animal, and to spot what is missing

To recognise animals and their babies

Playing with toy animals can reinforce children's experiences with the real ones.

WHAT TO DO

- Lay out the animals and talk to the children about each one in turn. Ask the children to draw the animals to encourage them to observe the animals closely and become familiar with their names and so on.
- Put some of the animals on the tray. Ask children to match the baby animals to their mothers.
- Cover the tray with a cloth. Who can remember which animals there were?
- Now take away one baby animal and remove the cloth. Can children guess which animal is missing?
- Share the story books, then let children make up their own games with the toy animals.

- Is it easier to guess which baby is missing or which mummy?
- Is it more difficult to guess if we muddle up all the baby animals or if they stand with their mummies?

12 Cuddly animals

1 4

Materials and preparation

picture reference of young animals · sugar paper or card · pipe cleaners · lolly sticks · scissors · sticky tape and glue · soft collage materials e.g. tissue paper, feathers, fabrics like velour, fur fabric, felt, toilet tissue · tin foil

To recognise animals and their babies. To recognise the properties of materials. To select and use tools and materials

To explore texture, colour and shape

Make collage cuddly animals with children and concentrate on how soft many young are.

WHAT TO DO

- Share the animal pictures. Let children choose their favourite to make a picture of. Talk about the body shape and parts of each animal.
- Talk about how their animal feels to the touch. Feel the collage materials. Which ones will be best? Will children need different materials for different parts of the body, e.g. fluffy feathery materials for a chick's body but a hard material for the beak.
- Give children sugar paper or card and help them draw and cut out the main head and body shape of their animal.
- Let the children choose the materials they want to create their animals.

TIP Use double-sided tape to stick the animals to cardboard tubes. They will then stand up and can be used to make an animal parade or to play with.

Younger children may find cutting card frustrating. Let them draw their own shape, then cut it out for them. Make sure they have opportunities to cut paper and collage materials.

13 I like spring

Materials and preparation

- read lots of different types of poetry to children (see resources)
- talk about what makes a poem (see section on poetry on page 8)

To respond to poems and rhymes.
To make up poems

To make decisions in a group

To express thoughts and feelings imaginatively

TIP If some of the children want to write a poem, but need more help to think up ideas, you could use this structure to give them a head start.

Even very young children can make up their own poems once they realise that poems don't have to rhyme. Start by making up a poem together.

Spring poem structure

I like spring because ...
and I see ...
and I can ...
and I feel ...
I like spring.

EXTENSION IDEAS

- Practise non-rhyming poems together to record or recite out loud.
- Invite parents and carers to come and see the children perform their poems.

WHAT TO DO

- Ask children to tell you what they like about spring and write down each word or phrase on a separate strip of paper.
- Decide together which order the strips should go in to make the best poem.
- Do children have a favourite phrase or word that could be repeated at the beginning and end of the poem?
- Always give children the opportunity to say if they don't like spring and why.

Questions

- What is spring like?
- How does it make you feel?
- What can we see/do in the spring?

14 Spring dance

Materials and preparation

- 'Spring' from 'Four Seasons' by Vivaldi
- CD or cassette tape player

To respond imaginatively to music and to express feelings

To move confidently and be aware of space and other children

To listen attentively and to join in group activities

TIPS

- Listen to the music several times before dancing to it and encourage children to tell you the spring events they think are being represented.
- Dance to the music several times encouraging different interpretations each time.

Once children have grasped what happens in spring, start work on creating a dance in which they can express what they've learned.

WHAT TO DO

- Build familiarity with the music both by listening to it and repeating the dance sessions over a few weeks.
- Look at your spring display and talk about what happens in spring.
- Explain Vivaldi wrote this piece of music about spring. Listen to it together and talk about the elements of spring the music reminds them of.
- Play the music again, this time, to dance to. Suggest they could be spring flowers opening, spring lambs frolicking, blossom flowering then falling to the ground etc. If children are confident, let them decide for themselves what they will do.

SUMMER

This chapter looks at summer, focusing on the warmth and long daylight hours of summer sunshine. An awareness of the seasonal changes in daylight and the sun's strength will be crucial for children's later learning, when they will begin to understand the changing seasons are being caused by the Earth's tilted rotation in relation to the Sun. The activities explore the summer weather and the effect it has on nature and how we behave. Many activities are based outside and encourage children to observe their natural surroundings. Picnics and sports day activities also highlight how summer weather differs from weather in the other seasons. In the light of recent research, the dangers of exposing skin to the sun are highlighted throughout this chapter.

Activities in this chapter

1
What is summer?
Using a 'feely bag' to help children focus on all the things we associate with summer

2
Summer begins with S
Giving 'feely bag' clues based on initial sounds and developing a display of things that begin with S

3
Sunny summer morning
Singing 'Here we go round the Mulberry Bush' but making some seasonal changes

4
Keeping cool
A sorting activity that helps children think about the way our clothing changes in the summer

5
Changing shadows
An activity that takes children out of the setting to look at the way shadows change through the day

6
Make a shadow theatre
Children play with shadows and discover the relationship between shadows and light sources

7
Summer trees
Going for a walk to look at how nature has changed provides a chance to print with leaves on their return

8
Beautiful butterflies
Children carefully observe a butterfly then try to create their own beautiful symmetrical patterns

9
Eating outside
Planning and eating a picnic provides an opportunity for children to think about how what we eat changes in summer

10
Cooking outside
A barbecue gives children a different experience of eating outdoors

11
Seaside role play
Recreate the seaside in your nursery and let children discover a whole new habitat

12
Summer sports
Plan a sports event with children and help them to recognise the importance of the weather in everything we do

1 What is summer?

Materials and preparation

- colourful bag large enough to contain a range of summer objects, such as sunglasses, bucket and spade, hat, tennis racket, model butterfly, postcard, holiday photographs, shell, large leaf. Ensure some of these objects start with 's' to use in next activity

To extend vocabulary, using discussion to clarify ideas and feelings

To work as part of a group, taking turns

To observe and identify features of natural events

Include objects with a range of textures and a range of made and natural objects. This will help prompt new language.

Use a guessing game to introduce new vocabulary and develop an awareness of what happens in the summer.

Never use a plastic bag as a feely bag.

EXTENSION IDEA

- Put all the summer objects together to create a What is summer? display. Photograph the display and use it when comparing summer with other seasons.

WHAT TO DO

- Talk about each object with the children. Ask them children to close their eyes, then put one of the objects in the bag.
- Ask the children if they can guess what it is just by touch. Ask them to describe the object.
- Leave the objects and bag out for children to play with by themselves.
- Encourage children to bring in objects from home to play the game.

Questions

- Introduce appropriate language, such as square, round, heavy, light, rough, smooth, spikey.
- What is it?
- What do we use it for?
- How does it make us think of summer?

2 Summer begins with S

Materials and preparation

- summer objects and bag as above

To work as part of a group

To hear initial sounds and link to letters

EXTENSION IDEAS

- Help children to cut out large S shapes to decorate with summer pictures from magazines and catalogues.
- Lay out one hoop and a range of objects, some beginning with S. Ask the children to sort the S objects into the hoop.

Use this activity as an extension to What is summer? (1) to build an awareness of initial letter sounds.

WHAT TO DO

- Play the feely bag game described above, but this time ask the child feeling the object to give the other children a clue so they can guess what it is.
- Start with clues on how it feels or what it is used for and then ask them to say the sound the word begins with.
- When you have played the game enough, ask children to sort out all the objects that begin with S.
- Make a display and ask children to add other objects from home or around the nursery that begin with S.

3 Sunny summer morning

1
WHOLE GROUP

To listen and respond to songs

To work as part of a group

To observe and identify features of natural events

To talk about events in their own lives

Change the words to 'Here we go round the Mulberry Bush' and encourage children to think of all the things they can do on a summer's day.

Here we go round the Mul- berry Bush, The
Mul- berry Bush, the Mul-berry bush, Here we go round the
Mul-berry Bush on a cold and fros- ty morn- ing.

Take this opportunity to remind children that early winter mornings are dark and early summer mornings are light.

EXTENSION IDEAS

This is the way we ...

- skip to nursery
- play outside
- put on our sun cream
- put on our hats

WHAT TO DO

- Ask which children know 'Here we go round the Mulberry Bush'. Can they sing it to you?
- Explain you are going to turn it into a summer song.
- Teach children two verses of the new song and then ask them to suggest their own verses.
- Discuss how some of the things you do may be exactly the same whatever the season, for example, brushing teeth and hair, eating breakfast.
- Prompt discussion comparing differences and similarities between summer and winter mornings.

4 Keeping cool

1 4

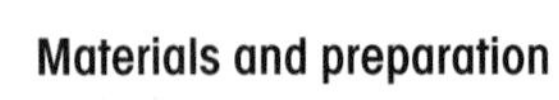

Materials and preparation

- selection of summer and winter clothes from a range of cultures
- suitcase
- washing basket

To ask and seek to explain how things work

To work together in pairs

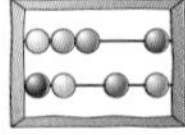
To sort things using different criteria

Use this sorting activity to talk with children about how we alter our clothing to suit the temperature.

EXTENSION IDEA

- Look at pictures of people in really hot places wearing hats or long trousers and sleeves. Talk about the dangers of exposing skin to the sun.

WHAT TO DO

- Ask the children what their favourite summer clothes are.
- Tell them you've been given some children's clothes and you want to put the winter ones away in the attic and wash the summer ones so they can be worn.
- Hold up each item and ask does it keep us warm or cool? What reasons do the children give?
- Ask the children to work in pairs to sort the clothes into the suitcase or washing basket.
- Let the children dress up in the clothes.

Children may assume that long sleeves keep you warm, so encourage them to think about the fabric and cut of the clothes as well.

5 Changing shadows

Materials and preparation

• large circle of paper with cross drawn in middle • marker pen • sunny day

To recognise time has passed

To explore and recognise shadows. To see similarities and differences and to notice change

To work with others

TIP Do this activity relatively early in the morning and late in the afternoon for the most dramatic effect.

Encourage children in the morning and afternoon sessions to work together to investigate change over time.

1 Stand on the cross. Ask one child to draw around your shadow. Annotate the time of day on the shadow.

2 Repeat with children in the afternoon. Stress that you are standing in the same place. Point out how the shadow has changed.

WHAT TO DO

- Talk with children about their shadow.
- Tell children you are going to try and experiment to see if shadows are the same in the morning and afternoon.
- Go outside and let children play with their shadows. Can they jump on each others'? Then follow steps one and two.

Questions

- Is your shadow with you all the time?
- What is the weather like when you see your shadow?

6 Make a shadow theatre

Materials and preparation

• light coloured sheet • 2 chairs • window with strong sunlight or a strong directional light • range of objects to use for casting shadows

To explore and recognise shadows. To find out how things happen

To take turns

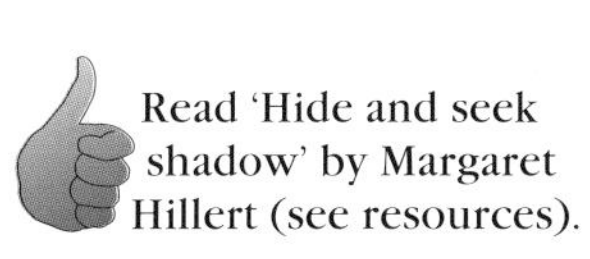

Read 'Hide and seek shadow' by Margaret Hillert (see resources).

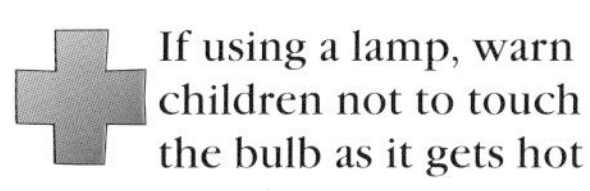

If using a lamp, warn children not to touch the bulb as it gets hot

Through playing with shadows children begin to understand that a shadow is caused by blocking light.

1 Demonstrate creating a shadow yourself first, so the children can see where you position the object in relation to the screen etc.

2 Show the children how to make the shadow smaller or larger by moving it towards and away from the light source.

WHAT TO DO

- Fix the sheet between the two chairs to form the screen. Place in the path of a strong light source (window or lamp).
- Make shadows with your hands or by holding up objects. Can the children guess what the shapes are?
- Now let one child take a mystery object into the theatre and ask the others to guess the object from its shadow.
- Challenge children to make their shadow shapes smaller or larger.

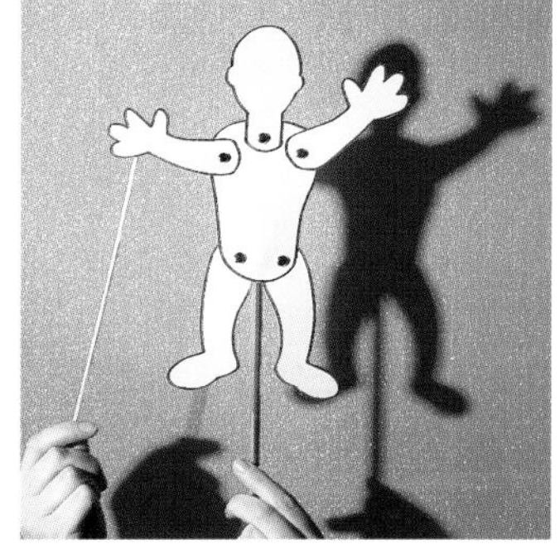

7 Summer trees

Materials and preparation

- large leaves which you have collected
- blue, yellow and white readymix paint
- thick paint brushes
- rollers

To explore the colour, texture and shape of leaves. To mix colours to vary the shades

To recognise different trees have different leaves. To learn that buds change into leaves

To recognise change over time

TIP To avoid smudging the prints set up two tables: one for painting the leaves and one next to it for rolling/ printing. Help children to carry the leaves between the tables.

Use leaf printing to see how the blossom and buds of spring have given way to summer leaves.

WHAT TO DO

- Remind children of the blossom they saw in the spring. How do they think trees look now?
- Take them on a walk around the trees in your locality. Stand underneath the branches and look up at the leaves.
- Point out how the sunlight gets through the leaf canopy. Notice how different trees have different shaped leaves.
- Back at nursery let children mix a variety of shades of green paint. Apply thickly to the leaves you have collected. Put paper over the leaves and use rollers to press down evenly. Peel paper back gently to see the leaf print.

8 Beautiful butterflies

Materials and preparation

- information book on butterflies, 'The Very Hungry Caterpillar', 'Amanda's Butterfly' (see resources section)
- butterfly/fishing net
- jar with lid with holes
- lettuce leaves for butterfly to feed on
- thin card
- thin elastic
- string
- collage materials
- brightly coloured finger paints

To learn that living creatures can change

To recognise change over time

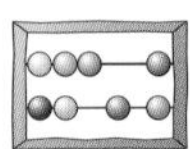

To recognise and recreate patterns

Make hanging butterflies to introduce the idea of the life cycles of some summer creatures.

1 Help children to draw and cut out butterfly shapes with matching wings. Ask them to paint and decorate the wings to match each other.

Plant buddleia to attract butterflies.

2 Fix thin elastic to the finished butterflies and hang from string stretched across the nursery.

WHAT TO DO

- Share 'The Very Hungry Caterpillar' and talk about caterpillars turning into butterflies in the summer.
- Read 'Amanda's butterfly' and talk about catching butterflies to look at. Ask the children what they will need. Talk about the materials required.
- Visit a nature reserve or insect house at your local zoo to see butterflies.
- Look carefully at the butterflies' wings and at other butterflies in books.
- Reinforce the children's learning by asking them to make butterfly pictures when they get back to the nursery. (See steps one and two.) Give them reference material to look at, such as DK 'Explorers Butterflies and Moths'.

Eating outside

Materials and preparation

- 'It's the Bear' (see resources) - ingredients for picnic food e.g. bread and fillings for sandwiches, mini pittas, pakoras, fruit, crisps, drinks - picnic crockery e.g. disposable plates, cups etc. - paper and pencils

To recognise people do different things when the weather is hot

To listen and respond to stories. To talk and write when planning a picnic

To talk about hot and cold and identify different textures and tastes

TIP Talk about all the cold foods you can have and the advantages and disadvantages of each, e.g. ice cream may melt, spilled squash could attract wasps or ants!

Plan and enjoy a picnic together. Start the activity by reading 'It's the Bear'.

TIPS Let each small group make or prepare something for the whole group. Encourage them to count and match one to one.
- Invite parents to join in the making and eating of the picnic. This is something younger siblings can be involved in, too.

WHAT TO DO

- Ask the children to share their picnic experiences with the group.
- Plan the picnic together one week beforehand.
- Talk about having a mix of tastes and textures in the picnic. Ask the children to suggest a range of food.
- Choose the picnic foods together. Remember to check for allergies.
- Make a list with children of all the things to buy. Include at least one thing to make even if it's only filling pitta pockets.
- Plan where the picnic will be and what to do if it rains or is very hot. What should children sit on? How can they be sheltered or shaded?

10

Cooking outside

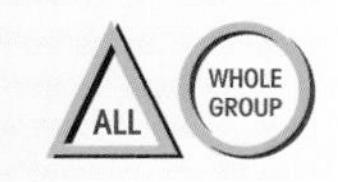

Materials and preparation

- barbecue - charcoal - fire lighters - tin foil - matches - kebab sticks/skewers - food e.g. kebabs, marshmallows, cubed meat, peppers, onions, cherry tomatoes, mushrooms, vegetarian burgers

To explore how things work

To understand different people like different food

To talk about and share past experiences

Warn children that the barbecue is hot. Never leave it unattended, even after you have finished cooking. Beware of ash blowing if it is windy. Don't sit too close to the barbecue to eat.

Follow your picnic with a grand barbecue and show children that even in hot weather we do eat hot food.

WHAT TO DO

- If you don't have an outdoor space, ask your local council for permission to have a barbecue in the park.
- Talk about cooking food outside. Look at the barbecue and discuss its parts.
- Look at and feel the cold charcoal. Ask if children have ever made bonfires or seen coal fires. Explain that charcoal is the fuel that burns.
- Involve children in the cooking by making kebabs. Cube meat and or vegetables and thread onto sticks or skewers. Cook over the barbecue.

Make a junk model barbecue for the children to use in role play.

11 Seaside role play

Create a seaside setting either inside or outside and have fun role playing.

Materials and preparation

- sand box • sand toys • beach toys and swimming things • paddling pool • seaside story books (see resources) • shells, gravel, pebbles or stones • plastic rock pool creatures e.g. crab, starfish • postcards

To understand different creatures live in different places

To take part in imaginative role play and to make up stories

To understand and use writing for different purposes

WHAT TO DO

- Make a 'sea' from blue cloth. Borrow an inflatable dinghy or air bed and add rubber rings and arm bands.
- Put sand at floor height. If you can't take the legs off your sand tray and don't have a sand pit, try to borrow one from the children. Add buckets and spades, flags and beach balls. Put the sand near to a water source or have a separate dry and wet sand tray. Wet sand is far more important at the beach than dry sand!
- Read beach stories and poems with the children then let them play and make up their own stories. 'If my dog went on holiday' lists all the things you can do at the seaside and is a very enjoyable read (see resources).

Make sure the children wear sun hats on hot days and talk about the importance of sunblock with them.

Let the children use the CD ROM 'Just Grandma and Me', in which the character goes to the beach (see resources).

If using a paddling pool, ensure the children are closely supervised at all times. Children can drown in the smallest amount of water.

Ensure the children learn the names of all the seaside props to extend their vocabulary.

WHAT TO DO

- Regularly add extra dimensions to extend the play – donkey rides if you have a rocking horse, real ice-creams one day, maybe even a Punch and Judy show!
- Make a rock pool by putting pebbles and shells in a bowl of water. Ensure the materials don't have sharp edges.
- Make a shop that sells sun hats, postcards and real ice-creams. Let children make items to sell, price lists and labels for the different items.
- Write postcards to friends and family from the beach shop.

12 Summer sports

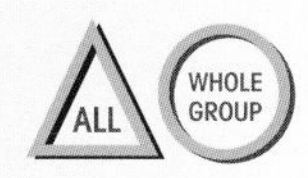

Materials and preparation

- television footage of sports events, try to include people with disabilities
- sports equipment

To develop physical co-ordination

To join in group talk.
To plan co-operatively.
To write for a reason

To understand different people are good at different things. To consider their own feelings and those of others

Make posters and invitations with the children. Encourage them to do as much writing as possible.

When children help organise and take part in a sports event they can see the importance of the weather and how it affects what we do.

TIPS

- Have plenty of water or juice available. Even if it's not a hot day children will get thirsty.
- Keep a camera to hand. You can use the pictures to prompt talk with children, to make a book or to bring out in the winter and compare the weather.

WHAT TO DO

- Talk about planning a sports event. Look at footage of different sports. Which ones usually take place in the summer in this country? In small groups talk about winning, losing and taking part.
- Discuss the merits of each type of sport children would like to include in terms of whether all children will be able to join in. Be sensitive towards cultural and disability issues.
- Invite a local athlete in to talk to the children about how hard they practise but don't always win.

TIPS

- Keep spare clothes to hand in case of accidents.
- Ensure your first aid kit is well-stocked and handy.
- Ask for extra adult helpers to supervise activities.
- Have contingency plans for wet weather.
- Ensure there is plenty of shade for the children.

Questions

- Have you raced or played competitive games before?
- What does it feel like to win or lose?
- What games (races or activities) shall we have?
- What will we need?
- What will we do if it rains/it is sunny?
- Who will we invite?
- What information shall we give them?

TIPS

- Plan a range of competitive, self challenging, team and co-operative activities.
- Decide if prizes for winners are appropriate. Consider having a certificate for all children taking part instead.
- Let parents/carers know how long the event will last and what they need to bring for themselves and the children.

AUTUMN

This chapter looks at autumn, focusing on changes in the natural world as trees and animals prepare for the cold winter. Autumn is traditionally associated with harvesting in the western world and although we can now have fresh produce at any time of year, it is still important for children to be aware of seasonal food since this is the basis for many of our festivals and traditions in autumn. The activities give children the opportunity to explore the world around them and then express their experiences creatively.

Activities in this chapter

1

What happens in autumn?

Materials and preparation

- bowls to collect blackberries
- walking sticks to hold branches down

To recognise changes in the seasons

To use writing for a purpose

To be interested and curious about the world

To understand that food comes from plants

Ask parents to go with you if you are going to pick blackberries. Can they remember blackberrying as children?

Take children out to buy or pick blackberries and collect other autumn items to see how nature is getting ready for winter.

EXTENSION IDEA

- Ask parents or grandparents to send in examples or photographs of home-grown produce.

Questions

- What do you know about autumn?
- What will autumn weather be like?
- What do you think comes after autumn?

WHAT TO DO

- Talk about changes children might have noticed in the weather and their environment.
- Talk about picking and eating fruit. Emphasise the dangers and the need for adult supervision.
- Ask children to tell you about signs of autumn they might see when you're out. Write down their suggestions and when you get back to nursery go through the list again. Tick off anything the children saw.

2

Blackberry and apple crumble

Materials and preparation

- filling – 450 g cooking apples, 450 g blackberries, brown sugar, 2tbs water
- topping – 150 g self-raising wholemeal flour, 50 g porridge oats, 100 g butter, 100 g brown sugar, 1tbs shredded coconut, pinch of salt

To work with other children

To explore and select a range of materials and tools. To notice how the ingredients change as they cook

EXTENSION IDEA

- Photograph each stage and make these into a recipe book. Let children work independently from the recipe to make their own crumble another day.

Use the blackberries you gathered above to make a blackberry and apple crumble.

1 Peel and slice the apples and stew in a saucepan with the blackberries until soft. Add sugar to taste.

2 Put the butter, sugar, flour and oats in a bowl. Mix it all together with your hands until crumbly.

3 Once the fruit has stewed, pour it into an oven dish and spoon the crumble mixture on top.

4 Bake the crumble at 180°C (375°F, Gas mark 4) for 30–40 mins. Allow to cool slightly, share the crumble.

WHAT TO DO

- Let the children do as much as they can themselves. They can try weighing, peeling, chopping, stirring, mixing and spooning the ingredients.
- Make full use of the opportunities for mathematical learning when weighing and measuring.

Ensure children do not use or touch the cooker.

Questions

- How much sugar/flour etc.) do we need?
- How have the apples and blackberries changed in the pan?
- What do they look like?
- How does the crumble mix feel? (Ask when raw and when cooked.)

3 Hibernating animals

Materials and preparation

• lift-the-flap books • 'Wake Up Bear' • non-fiction books about animals that hibernate, include: bears, doormice, hedgehogs, chipmunks, snakes such as adders, some butterflies (see resources)

To respond imaginatively

To listen and respond to stories. To understand the structure of books

To understand that food comes from plants. To understand different animals have different ways of living

To take part in group decision making

Read 'Wake Up Bear' and make your own lift-the-flap book to teach children how in autumn many animals prepare to hibernate in winter.

EXTENSION IDEAS

- Listen to 'Brown Bear Snoring' (a song) on the Early Learning Centre cassette tape 'Never Smile at a Crocodile'.

TIP On the last page, you could add a caption saying 'Who's asleep in winter? Not me!'

WHAT TO DO

- Share the book and talk about animals sleeping through the winter.
- Look at a range of lift-the flap-books and talk about making your own about hibernating animals.
- Let children come up with ideas. If they get stuck, you could write 'Who's asleep?' on the top of each page and have a picture of a hibernating animal under each flap.

Questions

- Where do you like to sleep?
- Shall we put a flap on every page?
- How many pages shall we have?
- What should be under each flap?
- Which animals shall we include?

4 Autumn secrets

Materials and preparation

• home-made book from previous activity • decorated shoe box • shoe boxes to decorate (one for each child) • collage materials for decorating • objects for children to choose e.g. photographs, special pieces of work, favourite story books, old coins, feathers, pretty stamps

To recognise changes in the seasons

To show an awareness of themselves, their likes and dislikes. To be aware that others are different

To explore different materials

Use this activity as a follow up to Hibernating animals (3) to reinforce the idea of preparing for hibernation and to promote planning and anticipation.

Encourage children to bring something from home for their boxes to make the activity more personal.

WHAT TO DO

- Share the home-made book with the children and remind them of why animals collect food.
- Show the children your special box and something you have stored in it for winter.
- Let the children decorate their own boxes and think of items to put in them. Ask them to think if the items will still seem special in winter. Remind them some items may go bad by winter.
- Remind the children not to put in anything they might need before winter comes!
- Remember to look in the boxes together in winter and discuss the contents.

5 Sleeping trees

Materials and preparation

• range of fallen leaves • thin card • pencils

To use descriptive words with accuracy to express thoughts

To recognise changes in the seasons

To draw around objects with confidence and accuracy

Collect autumn leaves and introduce the idea that the trees won't need them in winter when they 'go to sleep'.

EXTENSION IDEAS

- Children can pretend to be autumn leaves falling from trees in movement time.
- Talk about evergreen trees and how they don't loose their leaves in winter. See Evergreens (10) page 41.

WHAT TO DO

- Take children out to collect fallen leaves or ask them to bring some to nursery.
- In small groups, feel the leaves and discuss how they feel. Introduce appropriate language such as pointy, crunchy, soft, dry, reddy brown, bumpy.
- Let children draw round different leaves on thin card and suggest a descriptive word for each one. Annotate the leaves with the children's descriptive words.
- Thread and hang the leaves from branches or a hoop, or pin them to an autumnal coloured piece of fabric to use as a drape in the display suggested below.

6 The colour of autumn

Materials and preparation

• different shaped sponges • yellow, red and blue powder paint • mixing palettes • paint brushes • large pieces of paper • skeleton tree to decorate with the children's leaves

To name colours

To explore colour shades. To mix colours

To cooperate and work closely with other children

TIP Use double-sided sticky tape instead of staples to attach the leaves to the tree – this will ensure children can participate fully in the creation of the display.

After describing the look and feel of autumn leaves let children focus on their colour.

WHAT TO DO

- Look at the autumn leaves collected and made in Sleeping trees (5) and remind children of the words they used to describe them.
- Suggest making an autumn tree display. Sponge print the background together, using autumn colours. Show the children how to sponge print without overloading the sponges with paint. Then add a skeleton tree.
- Add the children's leaves to the skeleton tree and any autumn items the children have brought in, e.g. leaves, conkers, acorns etc. Add autumn stories, poems and information books (see resources for ideas).

7 Salt dough vegetables

Materials and preparation

- range of vegetables • mixing bowl • 325g plain flour • 225g salt • 1 tsp oil • 250 ml water • rolling pin • baking tray • paint • varnish

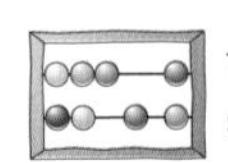

To estimate (and recreate) size and shape

To observe and talk about how things have changed

Look at vegetables then make salt dough models to introduce the idea of a harvest time.

Making dough

- Mix the flour, salt and oil together.
- Add the water until you get a dough consistency.
- Need the dough for 10 mins. Leave to rest in an airtight container for 30 mins before use.
- Bake the modelled dough for one hour at 150°C (300ºF, Gas mark 2).

TIPS Autumn vegetables you could show the children include corn cobs, carrots and brussel sprouts. You may like to include oats, barley and wheat ears, too.

- As harvest times around the world vary, talk to children about harvest festivals that happen in other seasons.

WHAT TO DO

- Show and discuss a range of autumn vegetables (see tips below).
- Talk with children about growing vegetables. Explain that, while most of these foods are in the shops all year round, they are harvested in the UK in autumn.
- Tell children about harvest festival (see resources for books).
- Suggest the children make their own salt dough vegetables. Use the real vegetables for reference.
- Bake the vegetables and when cool, let the children paint and varnish them.

8 Playing at greengrocers

Materials and preparation

- range of real or plastic fruit and vegetables • thin card • felt tipped pens • sticky labels • small chalk board • chalk • aprons • shoe boxes • scales • paper bags • shopping bags or baskets • purses • plastic money • till

To name fruit and vegetables. To take part confidently in role play. To communicate meaning through writing

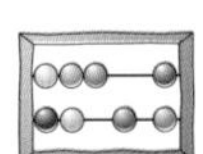

To weigh and count

To show an awareness of themselves, their likes and dislikes. To be aware that other people like different food

Reinforce the names of familiar vegetables and fruit and introduce some unfamiliar ones by turning the role play corner into a green grocers.

TIPS If you are using real fruit and vegetables encourage children to treat them gently to make them last longer.

- Try to buy quite robust things like sweet potatoes, carrots, oranges, kiwi fruit and corn on the cob.

WHAT TO DO

- Create a greengrocer's shop using a table with a table cloth draped over the front. Fix the cloth with tape or staples so that it doesn't fall. Use shoe boxes or tidy trays to hold the fruit and vegetables in the shop.
- Let children name each item whilst you label the front of each box.
- Ask children who are playing in the shop to set the boxes out on the table. Let each set of players write their own price list on card and encourage them to write and draw special offers on the chalk board.
- Talk with children about weighing the produce and about counting it.
- Extend the play by asking parent helpers to be the shop keeper.

Autumn festivals

Materials and preparation

- 'Rama and the Demon King' and other books on Diwali (see resources) • chalk • sugar paper • a paved surface • tracing paper • plastic shapes

To show respect for other people's cultures and beliefs

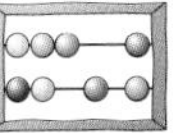

To recognise and recreate patterns. To name shapes

To listen and respond to stories

Mendhi (a henna like dye) is used to paint patterns and hands at Diwali. Use face paints to paint the children's hands. Don't forget to check for allergies.

Many festivals happen in autumn. Learning about a variety of them gives all children a sense of the richness of the cultural mix in Britain today.

TIP Rangoli patterns are used to welcome Diwali visitors. Let the children draw patterns in chalk on paving stones outside the nursery door or on sugar paper. Use paper patterns to decorate the nursery entrance.

WHAT TO DO

- This activity is based on the Hindu festival of Diwali. Invite a parent or leader from the Hindu faith community in to tell the story of 'Rama the Demon King'. Alternatively read the story to children.
- Talk about all the ways Hindus celebrate Diwali. Look at pictures of Rangoli patterns. Talk with children about the shapes and colours used and how shapes are repeated to make a pattern. Can children name any shapes?
- Give children plastic shapes to arrange into patterns of their own.

10

Pumpkin pie

Materials and preparation

For the filling: a small pumpkin • two eggs • 175 ml double cream • 60 g caster sugar • tsp ginger • 30 ml black treacle • ready-made shortcrust pastry • saucepan • potato masher • rolling pin • pastry board and cutter • spoons • four individual pastry tins

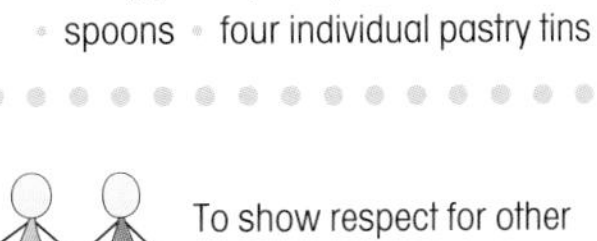

To show respect for other people's cultures and beliefs

To explore and select a range of materials and tools. To notice how ingredients change as they cook

Food plays a crucial role in children's lives. Associating special food with a celebration helps children to remember the festival.

Inform parents and carers beforehand in case of any allergies.

1 Dice the pumpkin and boil for 20 mins. Add the other ingredients. Let the children mash everything.

2 Show the children how to roll out the pastry. Give them a small ball each to roll out for their pie.

3 Help the children to line their greased tins with their rolled out pastry. Trim the edges.

4 Let them spoon the filling into the pastry cases and cut out leaf shapes to top the pastry.

WHAT TO DO

- To make pumpkin pies, follow steps one to four. Bake the pies for 40 mins at 180ºC (350ºF, Gas mark 4).

Ensure children are aware of safe practices when the cooker is on, and of the dangers of burns and scalds when cooking.

11 Rainy autumn days

Materials and preparation

- cassette player
- blank cassette tape

To use a cassette player and to understand how to operate it

EXTENSION IDEA

- Look for other nursery rhymes about rain: e.g. Incy Wincy, Doctor Foster, I hear thunder. Make a whole rainy day song cassette tape.

Sing 'Rain, rain go away' to raise children's awareness of how wet autumn weather can be.

Rain rain go away

Version one

Rain rain go away
Come again another day

Version two

Rain rain go away
Come on mother's washing day

Version three

Rain rain go away
All the children want to play

WHAT TO DO

- Sing each version of the song to the children.
- Have a show of hands to see which version is the favourite.
- Ask them to suggest other words that rhyme with away. Make a list.
- Take each word in turn and try to make a new song ending, e.g. stay 'we'll be sorry if you stay'.
- Children may offer endings that don't rhyme or scan very well. All contributions should be valued, but try to gently encourage them to hear the rhyme and decide which endings fit best.
- Record the children singing the new versions. Leave the cassette tape out so they can listen to it later.

12 Keeping dry

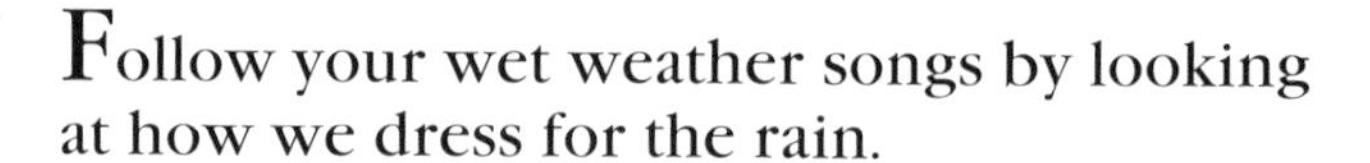

Materials and preparation

- wet weather clothes including boots, shoes, coats, umbrellas
- extra non-waterproof clothes for sorting, including swimming costumes, sun hats, towelling robes and jumpers
- 'Sonny's wonderful wellies' (see resources)
- watering can to pour water over clothes to test if they are waterproof

To try out ideas. To make connections

To explore different kinds of weather

To listen and respond to stories

To recognise and sort materials by their properties. To understand why we wear certain fabrics when it rains. To observe similarities and differences

Follow your wet weather songs by looking at how we dress for the rain.

WHAT TO DO

- Share the book. Talk to children about how much it has rained recently. If you are keeping a weather chart, count the rainy days.
- Ask what the children wear on rainy days. Make sure you allow children to simply say they have a coat with a hood, for example.
- Give children a pile of clothes and footwear to sort. Can they find things they think would be good to wear in the rain? Begin by asking them to close their eyes and feel the fabric each item is made from. Can they tell just by feel whether it will be waterproof?
- Go outside and test the clothes.

13 Autumn poem

To recognise changes and patterns in the living world around them

To listen and respond to poems.
To make up their own poems.
To talk about their experiences

Write the children's thoughts on the poem on the computer and give them print outs to take home.

Use this poem to re-visit the things children have learned about autumn and to let them talk about their experiences outside of nursery.

Before Winter

In Autumn
leaves swirl and twirl
to the ground
Golden brown and
fiery red
they rustle and crunch
as I kick them
Animals scurry through
the fallen leaves
Gathering food
to store somewhere safe
before the cold winter comes.

Sunny summer days
have turned into
chilly foggy mornings
Drumming rain makes
muddy puddles
that splash
as I jump in them
Birds queue up
on the roofs and fences
Waiting to fly off
To sunny places
Before the cold winter comes.

JO GRAHAM

WHAT TO DO

- Read the poem and ask children if they like any specific parts of it. Why?
- Are there things in the poem that they've done or seen at home or on the way to nursery? What do children think they've learned about autumn?
- If children are keen they could write an autumn poem of their own. They could use the leaf words they thought up to describe fallen leaves or write about splashing in puddles, for example.
- If any children have a favourite poem, ask them to bring it in and share with everyone.

14 Autumn sound effects

1
WHOLE GROUP

Materials and preparation

- range of percussion instruments, e.g shakers, maracas, guiros, claves, cabassas, drums, tambourines, glockenspiels
- range of materials that make noises, e.g: rustly paper, crisp packets, silver foil, plastic bags

To explore sounds.
To respond imaginatively to what they hear.
To choose instruments according to their sound

To listen attentively

EXTENSION IDEAS

- Record each instrument being played. Play the cassette tape to the children. Ask if they can identify the instruments and remember when during the poem they were played.

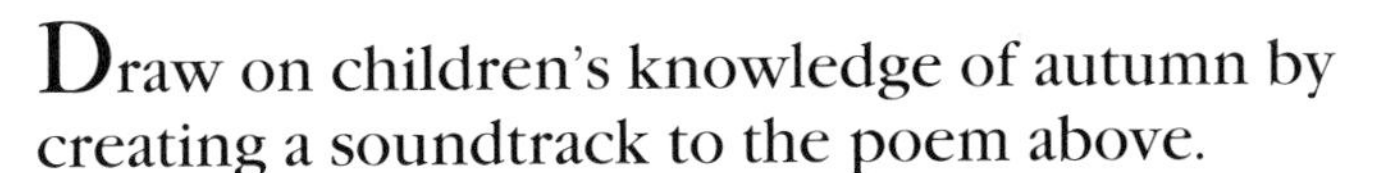

Draw on children's knowledge of autumn by creating a soundtrack to the poem above.

1 Hand out the instruments and remind children which part of the poem they are providing the sounds for.

2 Read the poem out slowly, pausing each time a sound effect is needed, and reminding children if they forget.

3 Let children do this as many times as they like and then give each group the opportunity to perform their version to the others.

WHAT TO DO

- Share 'Before Winter'
- Explain to the children they are going to add sound effects whilst you read the poem again. Ask which noises they think they can make.
- Begin by asking for volunteers to make noises with their bodies e.g. leaves swirling might be children rubbing their hands together, animals scurrying might be them clapping quickly.
- When children have identified all the parts of the poem that could have noises added, bring out the instruments and other bits and pieces. Listen to each instrument carefully. Can children suggest which, if any, sound effect it should be used for? Follow steps one to three.

WINTER

This chapter looks at winter, focusing on changes in the weather and how we can keep ourselves warm. Winter sees the end of the calendar year and the beginning of the new seasonal cycle. The activities allow children to experiment with ice, imagine themselves in snowy wildernesses and empathise with the birds and other creatures living outdoors in the cold winter. Children are also encouraged to think about how recreational activities vary in the winter months by comparing and contrasting indoor and outdoor games.

Activities in this chapter

1
What happens in winter?
A winter walk to encourage children to notice the changes winter has brought

2
Dressing up warm
This activity encourages children to think about how the weather affects how we dress

3
Hats and more hats
An experiment to show children how much heat we lose through our heads

4
Warm winter food
A simple cooking activity to help children think about the sort of food we like to eat in winter

5
The North wind blows
Say the rhyme and let children make up the actions

6
The Snowman
An art activity to make snowmen in response to the famous story book

7
Salty snow
Children explore an imaginary snowy landscape made of cooking salt

8
What is snow made of?
An experiment to discover that snow and ice are really the same thing as water

9
Winter trees
An art activity where children draw their own trees in response to works by great artists

10
Evergreens
Using their senses and talking about evergreen leaves, this activity encourages children to compare and contrast different objects

11
Outdoor games
A physical activity that keeps children moving outside to keep them warm

12
Indoor games
An activity to help children reflect on their own likes and dislikes and think about playing by the rules and taking turns

13
Bird feeders
An activity to make bird feeders that children can then watch and record the birds that use them

14
Chinese New Year
Creating a Chinese dragon and making up a dance help children to get into the swing of this colourful winter festival

1 What happens in winter?

Materials and preparation

• books and pictures of winter weather (see resources) • winter outdoor clothes

To dress themselves to go outside

To listen attentively and talk about their experiences

Questions

- How does the weather feel on the way to and from nursery?
- What's been happening to the trees, bushes and flowers now it's winter?

Take children on a winter walk and let them feel how cold the weather is in winter.

WHAT TO DO

- Look at the books and talk about winter weather.
- Go out for a winter walk. Encourage children to put on their own hats, coats, gloves and scarves.
- Point out frost, ice, bare trees and bushes and also evergreens.
- Talk about what you saw when you get back to nursery.

Ask parents to come with you. Use this opportunity to encourage children to talk confidently with other adults.

2 Dressing up warm

Materials and preparation

• 'Buster Keeps Warm' (see resources) • range of children's winter clothes • 5 dolls • dolls' clothes

To listen and respond to stories

To consider uses of different materials

To show increasing control in fine motor skills

Follow up What happens in winter? (1) by looking at how we dress in winter.

WHAT TO DO

- Share the book and ask children to name and describe the clothes they are wearing today.
- In groups of five, ask children to feel the fabrics of the children's clothes including hats, scarves, gloves etc. What do they feel like?
- Now look at the dolls' clothes. Which do children think the dolls should wear to go out on their winter walk? Let children choose clothes and dress the dolls.

EXTENSION IDEAS

- Send the dolls home with the children who dressed them that day. The next day the doll can 'tell' the rest of the nursery what she did on her adventure.
- If you send dolls home, don't forget to let parents know what the point of the activity is. Also have a clear policy on what to do if a doll doesn't return or is damaged in any way.

TIP Put up a notice asking parents to bring in their children's dolls and clothes to ensure you have a good selection for the activity. Ensure you note who brought in what so all items can be returned to their owners.

3 Hats and more hats

Materials and preparation

• selection of hats e.g. ski hats • swimming caps • emergency services hats • peaked caps • baseball caps • woolly hats, • fleece hats • fez • chef's hat • pictures of people wearing different hats

To join in role play

To ask questions about why things happen and how things work

Check for headlice before swapping hats.

Include a mirror, so the children can see what they look like in each hat and how it covers their head.

Play with hats and let children discover how much heat we lose through our heads.

Ask parents to bring in a selection of hats for the activity.

WHAT TO DO

- Ensure each child has a warm winter hat and coat for this activity.
- Talk about what the children wear in cold weather. Which piece of clothing do they think keeps them warmest?
- Take children outside to play for a few minutes with hats on but no coats. Now swap their hats for coats. Are they surprised at how warm the hats kept them?
- Back in the nursery, look at a range of hats. Which do children think would keep them the warmest? Let them pass the hats round and try them on.

4 Warm winter food

Materials and preparation

• baking potatoes, 1 per child • range of fillings e.g. grated cheese, tuna fish, sweetcorn, baked beans, mayonnaise • butter or margarine • fork • tin foil • round bladed knife • spoon

To handle tools safely. To work with malleable materials

EXTENSION IDEA

- Ask parents or grandparents from different cultures to come in and cook winter food from their own recipes with children. If they can't come in and help, they could send in their favourite recipes for you to try.

Always supervise children using graters. The potatoes are very hot when they come out of the oven.

Make jacket potatoes with a range of fillings and get children thinking about the sort of food we eat in winter.

1 Wash and prick the potatoes. Wrap each in foil and bake for one hour at 190ºC (375ºF, Gas mark 5).

2 Make the fillings. When the potatoes are baked, remove the foil and cut open. Add butter.

3 Add the chosen fillings. Baked beans are very quick to heat through and popular with children.

4 Other fillings may include tuna mixed with sweet corn, pepper and mayonnaise or grated cheese.

WHAT TO DO

- Talk about the kinds of food children like to eat in winter. Suggest making some filled jacket potatoes. Ask the children to list their favourite fillings and then decide together which to make.
- Encourage children to do as much as they can themselves with the exception of the stages involving the oven.
- Follow steps one to four to make the jacket potatoes with the children.

When the potatoes are cooked, allow to cool for a short while, then scoop out the flesh. Let the children mash the potato and add butter and then spoon it back in the skins. Younger children may need help.

5 The North wind blows

To respond to and join in with songs and rhymes

To work together as a group

To learn about the natural world

EXTENSION IDEA

- Ask children to make up their own actions to the rhyme.

Share this traditional rhyme about winter weather with children.

Cold winter

The North wind doth blow,
And we shall have snow,
And what will the Robin do then,
Poor thing?
He'll sleep in the barn,
To keep himself warm,
And hide his head under his wing,
Poor thing!

The North wind doth blow,
And we shall have snow,
And what will the children do then,
Poor things?
When lessons are done,
They will skip, hop and run,
To keep warm till Spring comes again,
Poor things!

WHAT TO DO

- Recite the rhyme. Have children seen a robin? Can they describe it?
- Talk with children about the rhyme. Do they know what a barn is? Where else do they think animals and birds could shelter from bad weather?
- Share the rhyme again as a group. Give children the opportunity to say it by themselves if they'd like to.
- Ask the children to think of other winter rhymes and songs. Sing them together.

If you did Sunny summer morning (3) page 22 in the summer, remind children of the words you sang and contrast the cool winter weather with the warm summer weather.

6 The snowman

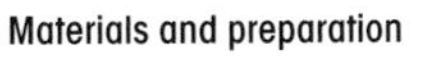

Materials and preparation

• 'The Snowman' storybook and video (see resources) • large pieces of dark coloured sugar paper • white chalk for the outline • white ready mix paint in flat trays • sponges cut into regular shapes collage materials • glue

To learn about events in the natural world, especially different kinds of weather

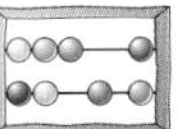

To understand the same size. To name regular 2-D shapes

To respond to and join in with stories

To work together in pairs

Use 'The Snowman' by Raymond Briggs to begin an exploration of snow.

WHAT TO DO

- Share the story book with the children. Can they guess what is happening? Now share the video.
- Talk about making the Snowman and the little boy's feelings.
- Ask pairs of children to make life-size snowmen. Lay one child down on the sugar paper and help the other mark where the head and feet reach. Help both children make the shape of the snowman's head and body to fit the marks.
- Let children sponge print the snow on their snowman outline. When dry let them add the features using collage materials.

7 Salty snow

Materials and preparation

- 'Kipper's Snowy Day' (see resources)
- large, shallow, flat tray
- cooking salt
- small world figures, trees and vehicles, especially bulldozer type machines
- white paint
- paint brushes
- sugar paper

To use imagination in fantasy play. To explore texture and materials

To play independently

To make up their own stories

EXTENSION IDEAS

- Cut out the handprint snowflakes and hang them from garden canes to make a mobile.

Make a winter wonderland and encourage children to let their imaginations take hold as they make up their own snowy stories.

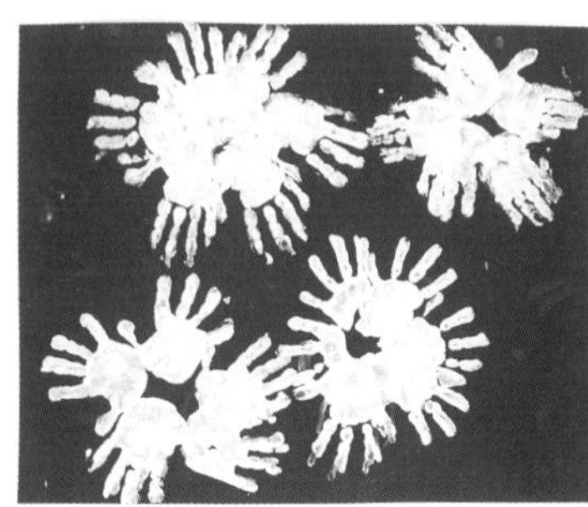

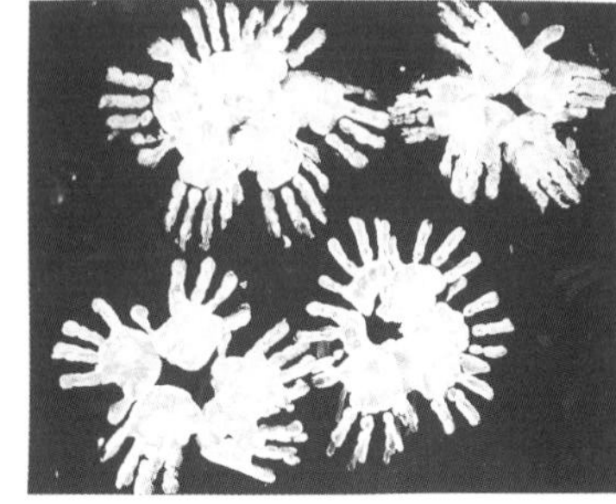

Ensure children know not to rub their eyes when playing with the salt and to wash their hands afterwards.

WHAT TO DO

- Read 'Kipper's Snowy Day' together. Talk about what you can do in the snow. Discuss the problems snow causes as well e.g. cars getting stuck, people needing to be rescued.
- Fill the trays 3/4 full with the salt. Explain the salt is representing snow. Show the children the small world toys. Ask what they could represent.
- Let children play in the snowy tray and encourage them to add other props as their stories develop.
- Let children paint snowy scenes with the white paint – they may like to make handprint snowflakes.

8 What is snow made of?

Materials and preparation

- snow/ice from outside or frost/ice from a freezer
- different shaped containers

To talk about their experiences

To learn about events in the natural world

To learn that water becomes ice when it freezes. To compare the properties of water and ice

Questions

- Introduce appropriate language, such as freeze, defrost, melt, thaw.
- When have you seen snow and ice? What was the temperature like when you saw it?

Explore snow and ice and let children discover that it is all the same 'stuff' as water

You could use shaped moulds to make the ice.

Ensure children know it is very dangerous to play near frozen ponds, puddles and so on.

WHAT TO DO

- Bring some snow or ice in from outside or take some frost or ice cubes from the freezer.
- Talk with children about when they have seen snow and ice outside.
- Ask children if they can predict what will happen to the ice in the warm room? What will be left?
- Once children have seen that the ice has changed into water, ask how they could change it back into ice again. Leave some water outside and put some in the freezer. Leave the outdoor containers overnight so children can see that it was really very cold while they were in bed.

9 Winter trees

Materials and preparation

• prints or pictures of paintings or other artworks featuring bare trees e.g. paintings by Pissarro, Monet, Pierre Bonnard and Corot • 'Wood' by Andy Goldsworthy 'Sisley' by R. Stone (see resources) • for wonderful textured bark show children the painting 'Grass in a park' by Van Gogh • sugar paper • brown or grey crayons and pencils

To explore shape, form, colour and texture in 2-D. To respond to a piece of art

To talk about their experiences

To marvel at the view of the world expressed in the artworks

Encourage the budding artists in your nursery and at the same time learn the names of the different parts of trees.

WHAT TO DO

- Look at the pictures together and talk about the different ways people have expressed what they saw when they looked at a tree.
- Visit a local bare tree. Talk about the branches, the twigs, the bark, the trunk and any dead leaves still hanging. Ask children to describe the elements. Feel the bark and any other parts children can reach.
- Does the tree remind them of any of the pictures they looked at?
- In the nursery ask the children to draw their own trees. Can they make the bark look rough? Let them use the pictures for reference.

10 Evergreens

Materials and preparation

• collect a range of evergreen leaves or boughs e.g. holly, ivy, fir • range of materials and objects e.g. tin foil, toy hedgehog, toothbrush, soft brush, smooth pebbles, dark green objects

To be capable of divergent thinking

To learn that not all trees lose their leaves. To recognise similarities and differences

To express thoughts and convey meaning in different ways

Use the exploration of evergreen leaves to encourage children to notice similarities and differences and extend their vocabulary.

WHAT TO DO

- Show the children the evergreen leaves and boughs. Talk about how not all trees lose their leaves in winter.
- Write down the words the children use to describe the leaves. Now ask them what else they can think of that fits each word, e.g. if holly is described as prickly, what else can children think of that is prickly? Can they find other things in the nursery or at home to go with the word?
- Make a display with each describing word, its leaf or branch and its set of objects. From time to time, play a game with children where you say 'Holly is as prickly as...' and they say something prickly they can think of.

Questions

- What shape are the evergreen leaves?
- What colour are the leaves?
- Which leaf is the darkest/lightest?

EXTENSION IDEA

- Older children could make simple poems based on the descriptive words e.g. Holly is as prickly/shiny as..., Holly is...

11 Outdoor games

Materials and preparation

- television footage of winter outdoor sports e.g. rugby, football, skiing, hockey

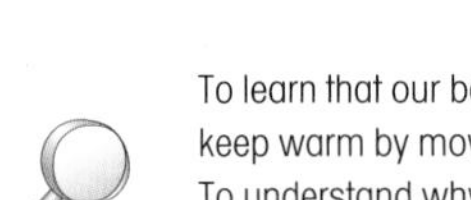

To learn that our bodies keep warm by moving.
To understand why games played in winter are physically active ones

Play a game outside to raise children's awareness of how moving about can keep your body temperature up.

EXTENSION IDEA

- Teach children different variations on the Tag game. Try cat and mouse where children are in pairs (a cat and a mouse) and the cat has to catch the mouse's tail (a ribbon tucked in a waistband). Alternatively, try colour tag where all the chasers wear a coloured sash or large sticker and all those being chased wear a different colour. When a child is caught they swap colours and become chasers.

Game rules

- Have 'stop' and 'go' signals that children recognise.
- For variety, the children could have to freeze in position when they hear the 'stop' signal.

WHAT TO DO

- On a dry but cold day, take children outside or to the local park or playing field and play the Stop and Go game (see Game rules, below left).
- In small groups talk about how warm the children got running about, even though it was a cold day. Look at the television footage of winter sports and talk about how much moving about the players are doing.
- Point out goal keepers jigging about when they're not actually saving goals or substitutes warming up and so on. Explain that they are doing this to keep warm, just like the children did when running around outside.

12 Indoor games

Materials and preparation

- 'Ten out of bed' (see resources)
- simple board and card games e.g. snakes and ladders, lotto games, snap, pairs

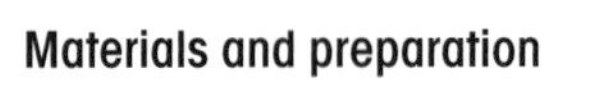

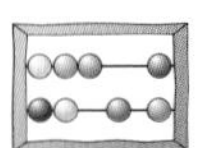

To match and count

To understand cause and effect

To take turns

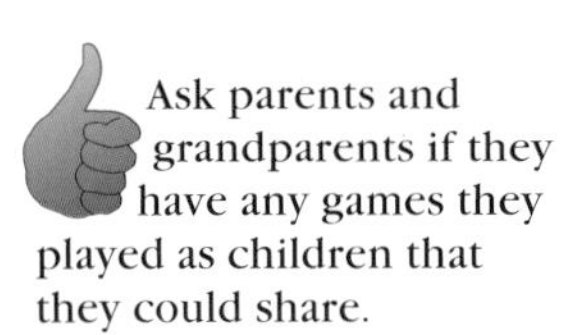

Ask parents and grandparents if they have any games they played as children that they could share.

Follow up your outdoor play by looking at games children can play inside when it's cold or wet.

EXTENSION IDEA

- Children may like to make their own games. Give them a blank 'race track' on a piece of card, with boxes marked out but not numbered. Children can fill in the numbers or colour the boxes and can draw pictures around some of the squares to show what will happen if you land on them.

WHAT TO DO

- Ask children what sort of things they do indoors at home when the weather is cold or wet.
- Talk about playing indoors. What are their favourite games? Read 'Ten Out of Bed' and talk about all the different ways people like to play.
- Organise a games session where children can choose to play board or card games. Ask parents to come in and help for this session, so there's an adult for each small group. Explain to helpers that they should begin by making sure all the children know how to play the game and understand the rules.

13 Bird feeders

Materials and preparation

- coconut • knife • string • bird seed and melted fat

To explore materials. To observe living things and to explore patterns and change. To talk about their observations.

To concentrate for a reasonable length of time. To learn to treat living things with care and concern

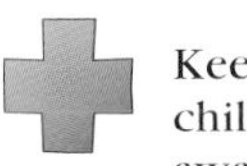

Keep children away from hot fat.

Food is often scarce in winter. Make bird feeders to raise children's awareness of this.

1 In advance, remove the white flesh from the coconut. Make two holes as shown above.

2 Attach string to the coconut through the holes so that you can hang the bird feeder outside.

3 Mix the bird seed with the melted fat. Pack this into the coconut and leave to set. Hang the coconut upside down for the birds to feed from.

WHAT TO DO

- Follow steps one to three for making a bird feeder with the children.
- Hang the bird feeder outside near a window so that children can observe the birds that visit it from inside the nursery.
- Encourage children to record which birds and how many visit the feeder. You could photograph the birds and put them in a home-made record book.

Make two bird feeders, one from each half coconut so that you can replace the first bird feeder with the second when it runs out.

14 Chinese New Year

Materials and preparation

- 'The Last Dragon' by Susan Miho Nunes (see resources) • Chinese festival music • long piece of light material • staplegun • green or red powder paint • tin foil • scissors • cardboard boxes • brightly coloured crêpe and tissue paper

To respect other cultures. To work together well in a group

To move confidently through space. To be aware of others

To respond imaginatively to music

Follow work on the calendar year by looking in more depth at a new year festival. Chinese New Year is usually celebrated around February.

1 Make the dragon's head and body from the boxes. Paint them green or red. Stick triangles along each side of the head for teeth and add the other features.

You could make the dragon's body from a large piece of fabric instead.

2 Cut holes in the head and body boxes, so the children can see out when wearing the dragon. Decorate the body with tissue and crêpe paper. Add red flames to the nose.

WHAT TO DO

- Talk about how Chinese dragons are used in street celebrations at Chinese New Year.
- Read 'The Last Dragon' to the children and then suggest making a nursery dragon. (The back of the book contains useful information about Chinese dragons.)
- Play children the Chinese music and encourage them to move around the room individually going up and down, high and low.
- Now let a group of children dance to the music wearing the dragon. Don't forget to photograph them!
- Ensure all children are given a turn.

EXTENSION IDEA

- Make dragon shadow puppets on sticks and let children dance their puppets to the same music.

THE YEAR ROUND

This chapter looks at the whole year, emphasising the order of the seasons and the fact that they always come in that order. The activities in this chapter are designed to help children develop a sense of time and raise awareness of the cyclical change that occurs in the world around us. There are also activities designed to help children think beyond their immediate environment and help them become increasingly aware that we are only living in one small part of the world.

Activities in this chapter

1
Your favourite weather
Sharing likes and dislikes about different kinds of weather

2
Make a weather chart
Developing observation skills by making a weather chart

3
A year in the park
Thinking about all the seasons, not just the current season

4
Adopt a tree
Studying the changes in a tree over the course of one year

5
A tree for all seasons
An extension to 'Adopt a tree'

6
The seasons game
A fun game to reinforce children's knowledge of the seasons

7
The colour of the seasons
Introducing colour association to children by looking at seasonal colours

8
The order of the seasons
Looking at different kinds of season display

9
Seasons' jewellery
Reinforcing seasonal colour by making jewellery

10
Which season?
A sorting activity concentrating on the differences between the seasons

11
Year round mobile
Looking at which months belong to each season

12
All the special times
Using special times to help to anchor events into seasons

13
The New Year
Looking at the cyclical nature of the year through children's birthdays

14
Weather round the world
Understanding the seasons vary around the world

15
Off on holiday
Reinforcing the idea that the summer season is popular for taking holidays in

16
Year round cookies
An enoyable baking activity to reinforce the seasonal learning in the activities in this chapter

17
Four seasons face painting
Face painting to symbolise the four seasons

1 Your favourite weather

Materials and preparation

- 'Kipper's weather' (see resources)
- finger paints

To name the different types of weather

To talk about their experiences

To know what they like and that other people are different

Share 'Kipper's weather' with children and see if they can name all the different kinds of weather.

EXTENSION IDEA

- Older children could take home a simple chart to fill in with their family. Each family member has their name in one box and one box to record their favourite weather in. Share the childrens findings in nursery.

WHAT TO DO

- Look at 'Kipper's Weather' together.
- Ask children which is their favourite sort of weather and why.
- Let children do a finger painting of themselves in their favourite kind of weather. What colours will they choose?

Questions

- Which weather do you think Kipper likes/dislikes?
- Which do you think is Kipper's favourite weather? Why?

2 Make a weather chart

Materials and preparation

- thick base card
- thin card
- wax crayons
- marker pen
- sticky-backed plastic
- Blu tac

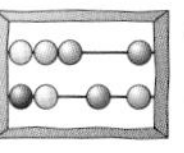
To name the months of the year

To know when their birthday is

To understand that the months of the year form a cycle

Questions

- How many days did it rain in (name of month)?
- How many days were sunny?
- Which month do you think will have the most rainy days? Why?

Make your own weather chart and use it to prompt children to see how the weather changes throughout the year.

WHAT TO DO

- Start by making a weekly weather chart and then create monthly overviews with the children.
- Talk about the different kinds of weather and make symbols together to represent them.
- At the end of each week add up how many days of rain, sun and so on there were. Do the same at the end of each month.
- Once you have built up a record over two or three months look at them together. Compare the weather between the months and talk about the seasonal changes.

Older children could record the weather on a computer programme.

3 A year in the park

Materials and preparation

- 'A Year in Percy's Park' by Nick Butterworth (see resources)

To listen and respond to stories. To listen and talk in a large group. To retell stories

To remember the characters and plots of a story over a period of days

To know the order of the seasons. To know the names of the seasons. To recognise seasonal change

Share the Percy stories with children to help give them an overview of how one place changes with the seasons throughout the year.

Ask a parent helper to make a story tape of the four Percy stories for children to listen to independently.

WHAT TO DO

- 'A Year in Percy's Park' has four discrete stories in it. Each story will provide enough to talk about in one single session, so start the book at the beginning of the week and read one story each day.
- Introduce the whole book to children in the first session and explain the idea of thinking about a whole year.
- Share the first story together and talk about it.
- In the next session ask children to recap what happened last time before reading the next story.
- As the week goes on children will be challenged to remember more stories and which season they relate to.

4 Adopt a tree

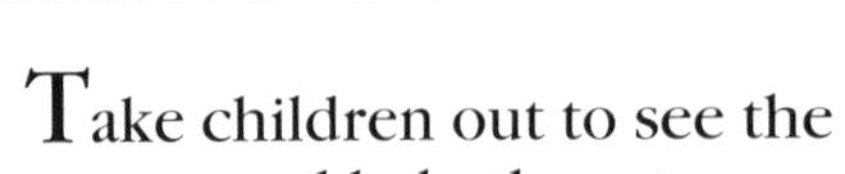

Materials and preparation

- camera • film • local tree • thin card • sugar paper • photograph mounts or corners

To remember and make links to earlier experiences. To make choices

To recognise and explore objects in the natural world. To be curious about the world around them.

To ask questions to find out why things happen. To compare similarities and differences. To use a camera

Take children out to see the same tree in each season and help them to compare their experience over time.

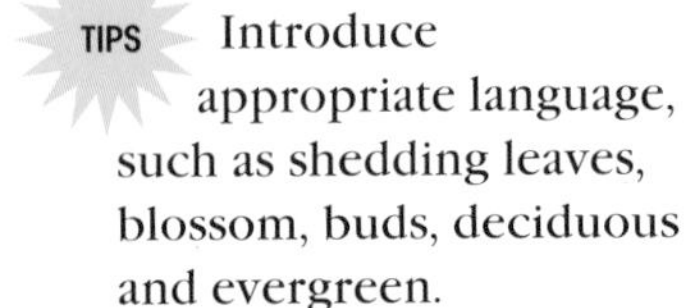

TIPS

- Introduce appropriate language, such as shedding leaves, blossom, buds, deciduous and evergreen.
- The children could draw the tree each season to complement the photographs.

WHAT TO DO

- Identify a broad leaf tree in a local garden, park or road that will shed its leaves in autumn and preferably blossom in spring (although buds will do).
- Visit the tree with the children at least once in each season and take photographs of it. Let children take their own photographs if possible.
- Make concertina books in small groups using pictures of the tree in each season. Each time you add a page talk with children about how the tree has changed.
- Let children choose their favourite photographs to add each time.

5 A tree for all seasons

Materials and preparation

- skeleton tree made out of felt on a felt background - selection of leaves, buds, blossoms etc made out of felt with Velcro on the back - woodland animal figures e.g. squirrel, mice, badgers, foxes and birds - thin card/paper - scissors

To work in pairs or independently

To make up stories.
To take part in role play

To know the order of the seasons. To know the names of the seasons. To recognise seasonal change

To use scissors safely and with confidence.
To use Velcro to fix pictures

This felt tree can allow children a more independent way to re-create what has happened to their tree.

WHAT TO DO

- Hang up the tree base and let children work in pairs to change the season. Work with them initially and then encourage them to work independently.
- Add plastic or cuddly woodland animals which children can bring to visit the tree.
- Let children cut out extra shapes from thin card or felt to add to the tree. These could be extra leaves, berries or fruit for the tree or birds' nests.
- Stick Velcro pads on to the back of the children's shapes so they can fix them to the tree.

6 The seasons game

Materials and preparation

- game board template on page 63 photocopied 12 times - crayons or felt tipped pens - 4 counters - dice - cup or shaker

To take turns and share

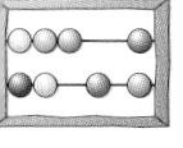

To count to 20

To recognise and explore objects in the natural world

To know the names of the seasons

Play this seasons game with children and reinforce the names of the seasons.

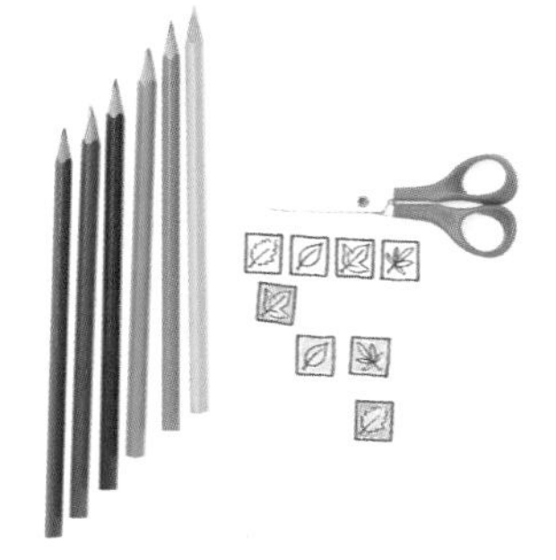

1 Photocopy the template onto coloured card and then decorate appropriately for each season.

2 Let the children colour in the counters. Older children may like to decorate the tree trunks, too.

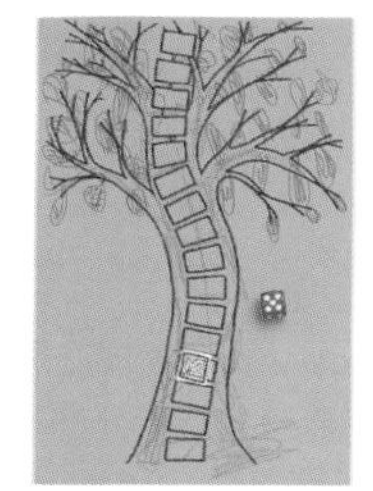

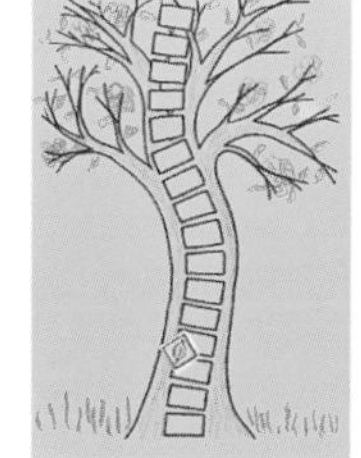

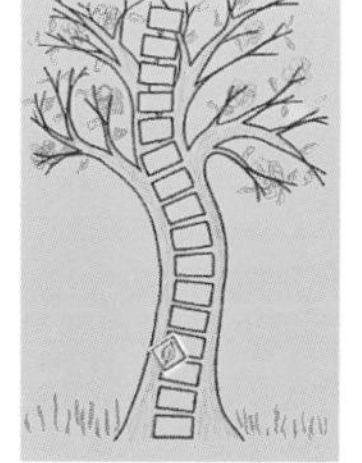

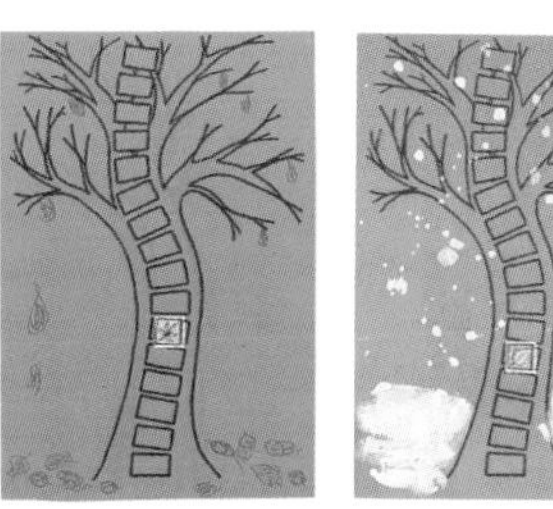

TIP Reinforce the seasons names by referring to each child by their season. 'It's winter's turn after autumn', 'Which season are you this time?' 'Would you like to be spring this time?' and so on.

3 You could ask a parent or carer in to help the children decorate the boards.

WHAT TO DO

- Follow steps one to three to prepare the board game. Write numbers to 20 in the boxes if desired.
- Divide children into groups of four. Let each child choose a board and a colour counter to match their season.
- Decide which 'season' should go first. Perhaps winter because January is in winter, perhaps the season you are in now. Make sure that the seasons follow in the correct order.
- Let each child roll the dice, count the dots and move their counters up the tree in turn.
- The first one to the top is the winner.

7 The colour of the seasons

Materials and preparation

• coloured paper • wool • strips of fabric • scissors • glue • glue spreaders • dowel sticks or string • sticky tape

To talk about their experiences

To explore colour and texture. To express feelings and ideas in an imaginative way

To work independently

To handle scissors safely. To spread glue without creating too much mess

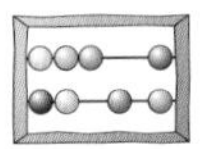
To use length words e.g. longer, shorter

Let children talk about their pictures at circle time.

Use this activity to build on the idea that we associate certain colours with certain seasons.

Niru
I think of yellow in the summer because the sun and sand is yellow.

Sam
I think of pink in the summer because my sunglasses are pink.

WHAT TO DO

- Talk with children about making their season picture. Ask them about the colours they associate with a particular season. They may, for example think of pink in spring because they see pink blossom.
- Give each child a piece of coloured paper. Let them choose wool and fabric to glue on it.
- Encourage children to cut the wool and fabric to differing lengths.

Questions

- What season picture would you like to make?
- What colours remind you of your season?
- Why did you choose those colours?

8 The order of the seasons

Materials and preparation

• large card circle • cardboard pointer hand • large split pin or blob of blue tack • catalogues • magazines • scissors • sticky-backed plastic • glue sticks or glue and spreaders • Blu Tac

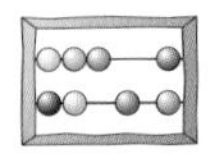
To sort into categories

To use scissors safely

To know the order and names of the seasons. To recognise events in the natural world. To recognise the cyclical nature of the seasons

To work in a large group

Make a huge collage season wheel to add to any season display.

Add the pointer arrow by fixing it with a split pin or blob of Blu Tac.

WHAT TO DO

- Name the seasons then ask the children to help you make a season wheel to display their seasonal work in.
- Divide the card circle into quadrants and write the season in each.
- Ask children to suggest the kinds of picture they could draw or cut out for each season.
- Divide the children into groups to look for season pictures and stick them on the appropriate part of the wheel.
- Let the children make the collage independently. Any glaring mistakes can be pasted over if necessary or may provide a useful talking point.

Season's jewellery

Materials and preparation

• plastic coated string or round shoe laces • things to thread e.g. pasta tubes or quills • white, yellow, green, orange, pink straws • wooden beads, variety of colours • buttons with large holes, include brown • cotton reels • milk bottle tops with holes punched through • feathers and other natural objects • sticky tape to attach feathers

To talk about their experiences. To name colours

To explore colour and texture. To express feelings and ideas in an imaginative way

To thread things confidently

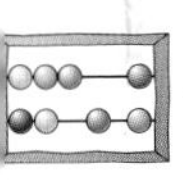
To use length words e.g. longer, shorter and position words e.g. next to. To recognise and recreate patterns

To work independently

Make jewellery and let children explore the associations they have developed with each season.

WHAT TO DO

- In small groups ask children to choose whether to make a spring, summer, autumn or winter necklace, headband or bracelet.
- Give each child a pre-cut length of string or lace with a knot tied in the end, so the beads won't slide off the other end.
- Let the children thread their chosen objects to make their jewellery. They will need to cut straws to the correct length.
- Tie the end for them and let them take their necklaces home.

Questions

- What colour objects will you need for your chosen season?
- Why have you chosen those particular colours?
- What does your jewellery remind you of/make you think of?
- Would you like to make some jewellery for someone in your family? Who and why?

Ensure the children are supervised at all times when handling small objects that could be swallowed.

EXTENSION IDEAS

- Can children make a repeating pattern necklace e.g. pasta then straw, pasta then straw?
- Talk with children about a celebration that falls within their necklaces' season. Add a centre piece to match the season, e.g. a moon for Eid-ul-Fitr.

Some children may enjoy making earrings to complement their necklace and or bracelet.

TIP To avoid gender stereotyping, ensure boys are actively encouraged to participate in this activity. If you can get a father or male carer to come and help, this will provide a positive role model for the children.

10 Which season?

Materials and preparation

- 4 large hoops
- pictures and objects to sort such as natural objects e.g. conkers, fir cones, green or brown leaves
- plastic or fabric flowers e.g. daffodils, roses, tulips
- cuddly or plastic animals e.g. lambs, piglets, chicks
- empty sun cream bottles, sun glasses and other summer objects
- winter and summer landscapes

To work in a small group or independently

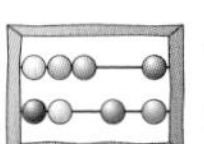

To sort and match objects and pictures

To recognise objects and events in the natural and made world

Use this sorting activity to encourage children to make connections and spot the odd one out.

Make a collection of just one item across all seasons e.g. shoes. Include unusual objects e.g. snowshoes, flippers.

Share 'My Season' (see resources) and talk with children about all the things they like doing in each season.

WHAT TO DO

- Lay out the four hoops, explaining each one represents a season.
- Give children a range of pictures and objects and ask them to sort them into the four hoops.
- Ask them to look away and then move an item across the hoops, e.g. a winter object into the summer hoop.
- Tell children there's something odd in the summer hoop and see if they can work out which item doesn't belong.
- If children become very good at this, ask them to work in pairs and make the switch for their friend

11 Year round mobile

Materials and preparation

- coloured card
- plate to draw around for ring
- marker pen
- scissors
- hole punch
- cotton thread

To recognise and explore objects in the natural world. To know the names of the months. To begin to develop a sense of time

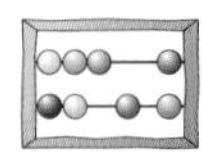

To sort, order and count

Raise children's awareness of what makes a year, the names of the months, and which season each month belongs to by making a mobile.

WHAT TO DO

- Talk with children about the months of the year.
- Follow steps one to three for making the mobile.
- With the mobile, play guessing games such as removing a month and seeing if children can guess which has gone.

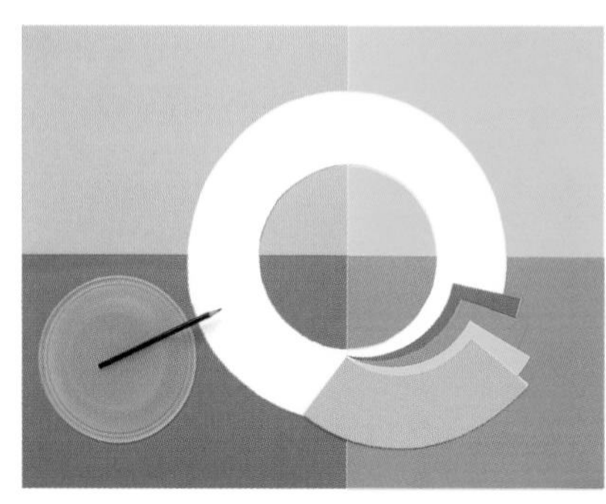

1 Trace around a plate to make a ring out of four pieces of coloured card - each colour representing a different season.

2 Make month labels that correspond with the colour of the appropriate season. Let the children help by naming the months in order.

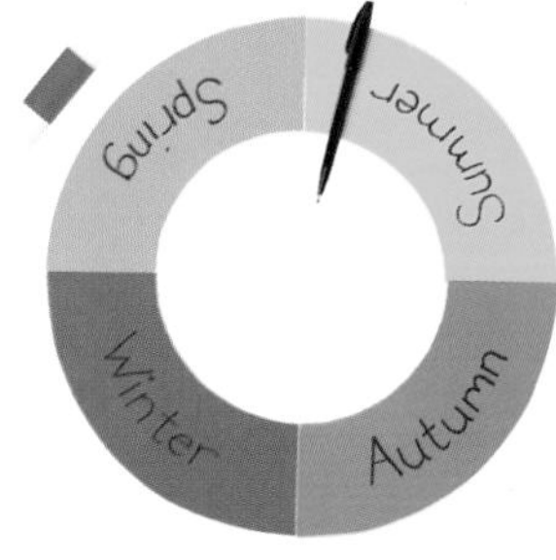

3 Name each season colour on the ring and then hang the month labels with cotton from the ring. Children may like to decorate the ring, too.

4 Look at the mobile together and discuss which months fall in each season. Encourage children to see that there are many 'cross over' months.

EXTENSION IDEAS

- Add month names in different languages.
- Share 'When the Wind Stops' (see resources) to help the children see how all the seasons fit together to make a year.

12 All the special times

Materials and preparation

- shoe box marked 'Things to look forward to'
- small pieces of paper
- marker pen
- 4 envelopes marked with the seasons

To sense anticipation and excitement. To share their feelings appropriately

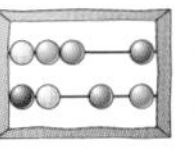

To order and sort according to set criteria

To begin to develop a sense of time

To talk about events in their own and their families' lives

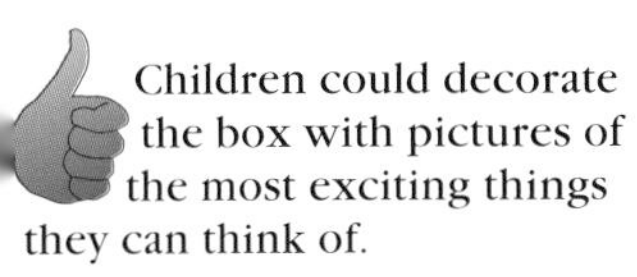

Children could decorate the box with pictures of the most exciting things they can think of.

Harness the natural sense of excitement children have about birthdays, holidays and other special events to develop a sense of time and to reinforce the order of the seasons.

WHAT TO DO

- Talk about all the special times that happen every year.
- Let children suggest events and if possible the month or season in which they happen. Write these down or let children draw them.
- Ensure that everyone has included their birthday.
- Sort all the events into seasons with the children and put them in the appropriate envelopes.
- Put the envelopes in the box. Add items as new children join nursery or children learn about new festivals
- From time to time, get the box out and talk to children about what they are looking forward to.

13 The New Year

WHOLE GROUP

Materials and preparation

- calendar with one page per month, preferably with a picture per month
- collage materials to make a nursery wall calendar
- children's work to decorate the calendar

To understand that the months of the year form a cycle

To know when their birthday is

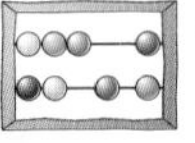

To name the months of the year

Putting children's birthdays on a calendar gives you the opportunity to show children that the new calendar year starts in January.

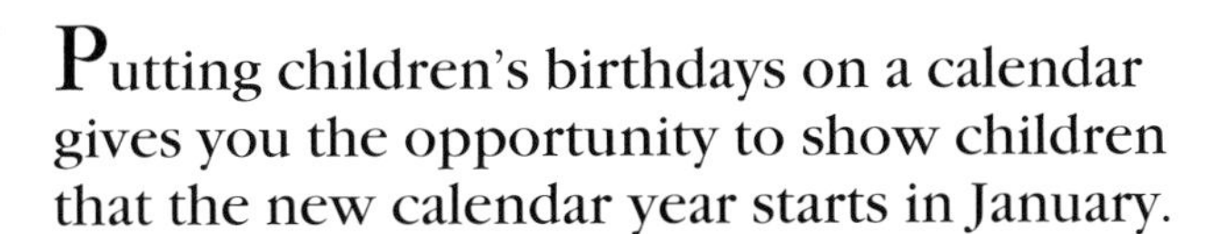

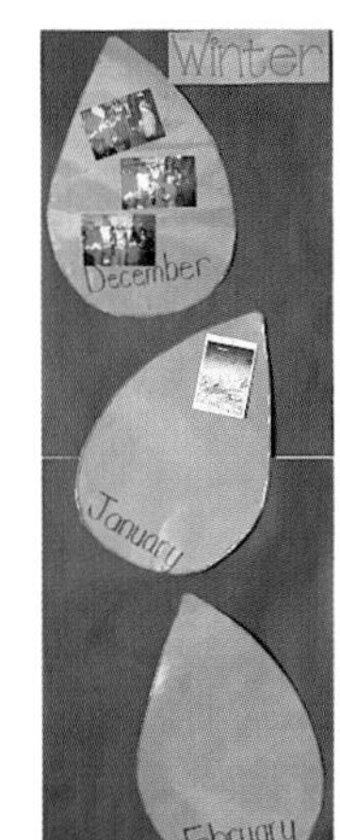

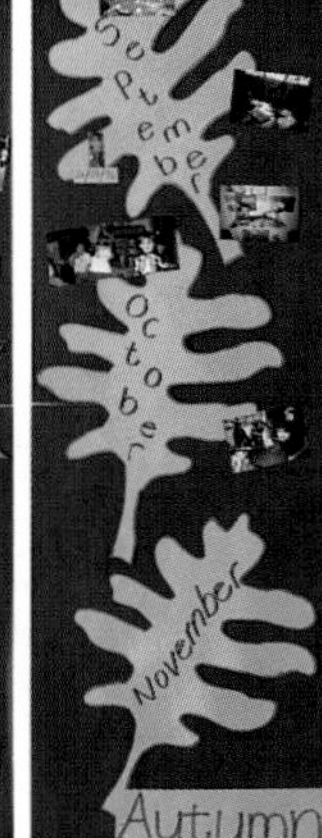

WHAT TO DO

- As a group look at the calendar for the new year. Read the name of each month out as you turn the page.
- Ask each child in turn to tell you which month their birthday is and write it on the appropriate date. If they know the day as well as the month, you could add this, too.
- Read through the months again. As you say each month ask children to stand up if that is the month of their birthday.
- Make a nursery calendar, adding children's artwork. You could divide the months into seasons to reinforce previous learning.

EXTENSION IDEA

- Talk about New Year celebrations. Did children celebrate new year in any way? Are any of the children in your nursery going to celebrate new year at a different time e.g. Chinese, Jewish and Muslim communities use a lunar calendar.

14 Weather round the world

Materials and preparation

• books showing pictures of different places around the world • television weather forecast footage • UK maps • world maps • globes • computer and internet access

To recognise features of the world and their own environment

To talk about their experiences

To remember and make links to earlier experiences

Use this activity to encourage children to realise that there are many places in our world that have very different weather patterns and climate.

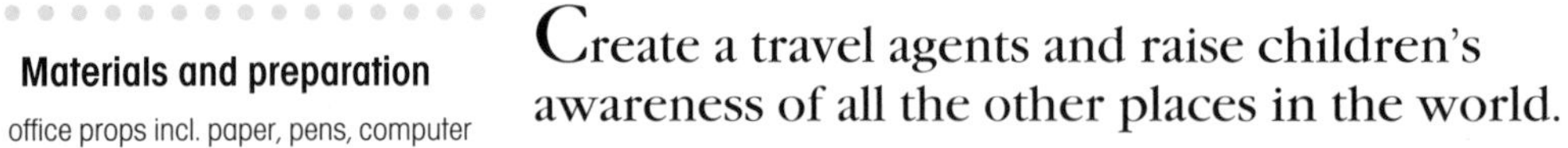

EXTENSION IDEA

• Children with family and friends around the world could write or e-mail them to find out what the weather is like there. Or you could e-mail a nursery in another country.

TIP Tape record television weather forecasts and show them to the children. Some forecasts e.g. show weather maps right across Europe .

WHAT TO DO

- Ask children if they can remember the names of any places they have been to. Remember that young children are still developing a sense of the relative size of places and America may be mentioned in the same breath as a popular theme park!
- Find the places on UK maps or on the globe or world maps.
- Do any children have friends or relatives in other countries? Find these places on the map.
- Look at pictures of different places around the world. Talk about the weather in each place. Include places like Australia which has summer when we have winter.

15 Off on holiday

Materials and preparation

• office props incl. paper, pens, computer or type writer, forms, till, telephone etc. • posters showing a range of climates and holiday activities • globes and maps • holiday brochures • holiday props incl. cases and bags, sunglasses, passports, a range of clothing, purses, camera etc.

To recognise and explore events in the natural world. To be aware of other places

To make up their own stories. To take part in role play. To write for different purposes. To be aware of print

To be tolerant and understanding of others

To respond imaginatively to what they see and hear

Create a travel agents and raise children's awareness of all the other places in the world.

Visit a travel agents with the children. Arrange the visit in advance, so it will be quiet and the staff will have time to talk with the children.

WHAT TO DO

- Create the travel agents using the materials listed.
- Visit a travel agents to find out what they do and collect brochures.
- Children may still need help envisaging what a travel agent does. Ensure an adult takes the role of the agent the first few times children play in the shop until they feel confident they can take on the role.
- Encourage children to not only choose, book and pay for their holiday but to pack their things and go!
- After each session ask children which holiday they chose or sold. Can they show you where they went on the map? Is there a favourite destination?

16 Year round cookies

Materials and preparation

- scales or measuring cone • mixing bowl • wooden spoon • metal spoon • sieve • rolling pin • oven • 100g butter • baking powder • 100g brown sugar • 1 egg • 225g plain flour • currants, cherries etc.

To work as part of a small group and independently

To handle appropriate tools and malleable materials safely and with increasing control

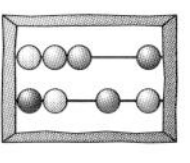

To weigh, measure and count

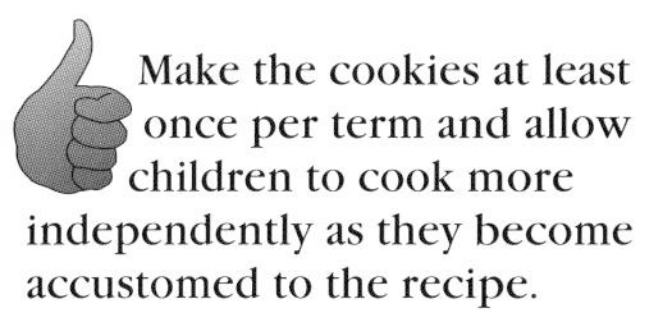

Make the cookies at least once per term and allow children to cook more independently as they become accustomed to the recipe.

Use this tried-and-trusted recipe throughout the year to make cookies that can be shaped or decorated to fit the season.

1 Mix the flour, sugar and baking powder. Add the butter and mix until it looks like breadcrumbs.

2 Whisk the egg and add it to the mixture. Mix it all together to form a ball of dough.

3 Roll out the dough and cut out a variety of shapes. Bake the shapes for 15 mins at 170°C (325/350°F, Gas mark 3).

WHAT TO DO

- Talk to the children about things that remind them of specific seasons. They may suggest flowers for spring or leaves for autumn.
- Introduce the idea of making cookies and decorating them with a seasonal theme.
- Talk with children about the shape or decoration that you're aiming for with the cookies before you start.
- Follow steps one to four to make the cookies, ensuring children do as much as possible themselves.

4 Decorate the biscuits with coloured icing and marzipan. You may like to add cherries or sugar flowers to finish

17 Four seasons face painting

Materials and preparation

- face paints and sponges • baby lotion to protect face before painting and to remove face paints • cotton wool to help remove face paints

To talk about their experiences

To explore colour and shape. To use a range of materials and resources

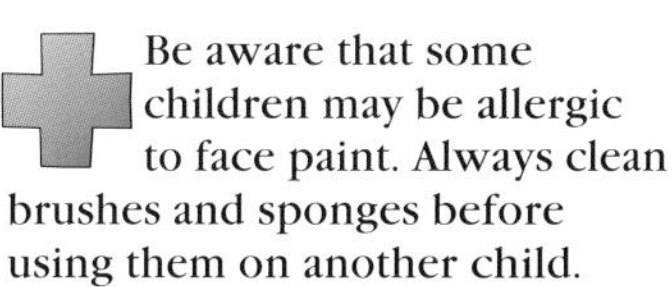

Be aware that some children may be allergic to face paint. Always clean brushes and sponges before using them on another child.

Reinforce seasonal learning by holding a face painting day. If you're artistic, give children free choice of how they'd like their faces painted, otherwise give them a menu to choose from.

Inform parents about the activity in advance – some may want to help and others may want to send their children in different clothes.

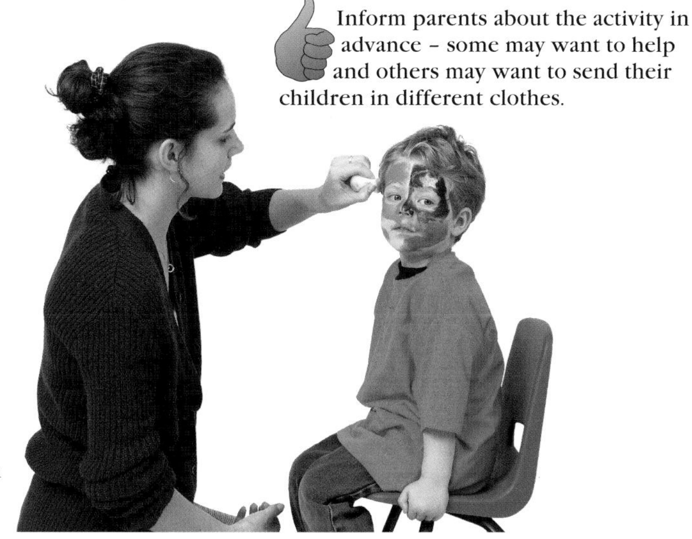

WHAT TO DO

- The simplest and quickest faces involve painting pictures onto cheeks, chins and foreheads. For a more complicated effect sponge base colour over the whole face.
- Older children may like to paint simple shapes like rainbows or suns on friends faces. Let younger or less confident children paint shapes or patterns on the backs of their hands.
- Keep a mirror to hand, so children can see their painted faces.
- Ask children for suggestions of something to paint from each season.

SIGNS OF CHANGE

This chapter looks at the idea of change in relation to seasons. The seasons change in a predictable order each year and there are signs of change both in and between seasons. Children at this age are beginning to develop a greater awareness of time and will be able to recognise the noticeable differences between summer and winter, and should be able to recognise differences between spring and summer, summer and autumn and so on. The activities in this chapter focus on recognising and observing changes in the natural world so that children can develop their awareness of changes within seasons and from one to the next. Finally, they will learn to recognise that these changes affect us, too.

Activities in this chapter

1
Looking for signs of change
Go outside with children and look at how the world around them is changing with the seasons

2
Snowdrops and crocuses
Children use oil pastels to create beautiful spring flowers; the first signs of spring

3
Roots and shoots
Children grow their own hyacinths and become aware that changes are happening all around them, even when they aren't visible

4
Growing movements
Create a dance to focus children on the way a plant changes as it grows

5
Days are changing
An activity to help children remember how dark it was in winter mornings and compare it to bright, summer mornings

6
How do you feel today?
An activity to help children understand that the weather can affect the way we feel

7
Life cycles
Playing with toys and games can help children to learn the language and sequence of the life cycles of some animals

8
How have you changed?
Making a scrap book charting their progress over the year can help children to reflect on the ways that they have changed

9
Musical change
A musical activity to help children represent a whole year in sounds

1 Looking for signs of change

Materials and preparation

- 'Changes, changes' by Pat Hutchins (see resources)

To respond to stories and books

To recognise and explore things in the made and natural world. To compare similarities and differences, to notice patterns and change

Take children out of the setting to explore the outdoors during and at the end of each season to look for signs of change.

Let parents know what you are doing and encourage them to point out changes to the children, too.

EXTENSION IDEAS

- Make a scrap book for each season. Include photographs and items you collected on your visits. Before you go out for each walk, use the scrap book to remind children what they saw last time. This is also a good way to introduce new children to the activity.

WHAT TO DO

- Share 'Changes, Changes' with the children. Talk about what has changed on each page. As children get the idea of the book, ask them if they can predict how the building will change in response to the events that are happening.
- Ask the children if they have noticed any things that have changed recently on their way to the setting. These could be natural or from the made world, e.g. a new building.
- Take children out regularly for walks around the neighbourhood. Direct their attention toward things you know will change over time, e.g. trees, plants, building sites, shop windows.

2 Snowdrops and crocuses

Materials and preparation

- snowdrops and crocuses in flower, perhaps in a bowl
- light coloured oil pastels
- dark sugar paper

To explore colour, shape and different media to express what they see

To recognise and explore living things. To compare similarities and differences. To notice patterns and change

TIP If this is the first time children have used oil pastels let them try the pastels out on a small piece of sugar paper first to see what effects they can make with them.

Develop children's observational skills by becoming nature detectives and looking for signs of child in the natural world.

1 Talk about which pastels the children think they might use. Give them pastels and sugar paper and ask them to draw the flowers.

2 Remind them that oil pastels can be smudgy which gives a nice effect, but can be messy. Let them experiment blurring the pastels.

WHAT TO DO

- Each season has its own signs of change. Here, we use snowdrops and crocuses to show how to encouarge children to notice that spring is on its way.
- Look at the flowers and talk about other flowers and plants children have noticed in bloom.
- Explain snowdrops and crocuses are usually the first flowers to bloom and are seen as a sign that spring is on the way.
- Help children observe the colour, shape and feel of the flowers. Follow steps one and two to encourage children to draw their observations.

3 Roots and shoots

Materials and preparation

- hyancith glass or clear containers
- hyacinth bulbs
- water

To recognise and explore objects in the natural world. To notice change over time.

To be curious about the world around them. To ask questions to find out why things happen

To take care of living things

To name the parts of a plant

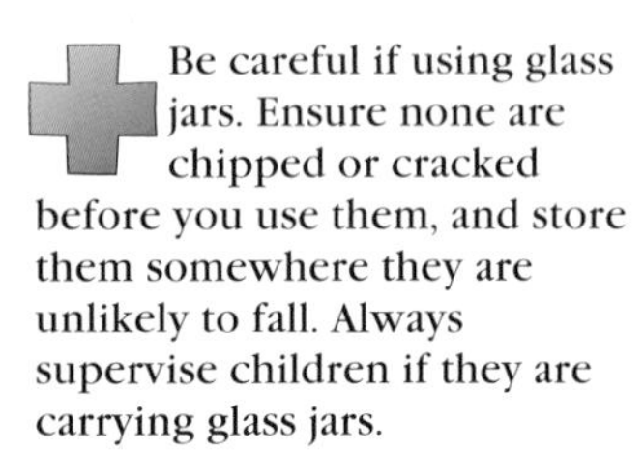

Be careful if using glass jars. Ensure none are chipped or cracked before you use them, and store them somewhere they are unlikely to fall. Always supervise children if they are carrying glass jars.

Grow hyacinth bulbs on top of glass jars and show children that there are changes taking place all around us that we can't normally see.

1 Put one bulb on top of each container filled 7/8 with water. The bulbs should be just above the water, as moisture triggers growth.

2 Leave the bulbs for approximately 10 weeks until first, the roots have developed and then the shoots have appeared.

3 Transfer the bulbs into plant pots with soil or compost and send home with the children as winter festival gifts.

TIPS

- Planting bulbs in mid October should give you a flowering bulbfor Christmas.
- Although the bulbs will probably flower left on the glass containers, they will become top heavy and may topple over.

WHAT TO DO

- Start this activity any time from September onwards.
- Follow steps one to three to grow the bulbs.
- Place the bulbs and containers where children can see them (but not reach them if using glass) and encourage children to check daily for signs of change. You could keep a nursery record book to remind the children of the changes.
- Talk with children about what they expect will happen to the bulb. Explain that normally these bulbs are planted under the ground but that the development process children will see is exactly the same as what happens beneath the soil.

4 Growing movements

Materials and preparation

- hyacinth bulbs with roots and shoots grown

To name the parts of living things. To understand that living things grow

To be aware of space and other children when moving

To use movement to express feelings or ideas

EXTENSION IDEA

- Listen to a range of classical music e.g. Bach, Sibelius and Tchaikovsky. Let the children choose which they think best fits the bulb's growth.

This movement activity can be used as a follow up to Roots and shoots (3).

If you have access to a camcorder or video camera, you could record the children's movement for them to watch later.

WHAT TO DO

- This activity gives children the opportunity to express what they have seen the hyacinth bulb do through dance and movement.
- Talk with children in a large group about the things they noticed the hyacinth bulb doing.
- Emphasise how slowly it grew and reinforce the vocabulary of the root and the shoot.
- Note down any words or phrases that children use to describe the bulbs and use them in your movement time.
- Encourage children to begin by curling up small and stretching out a root very slowly, then maybe sprouting a leaf.

5 Days are changing

Materials and preparation

- concertina books with 4 pages
- 3 times of day marked on each page e.g. 7.30am, when you get up, midday when you have lunch, 7.00pm when you go to bed
- 3 windows on each page

To write for different purposes. To make their own books

To remember and make links with earlier experiences

To recognise and explore events in the natural world. To ask questions to find out why things happen and how things work.

To compare similarities and differences. To record observations

To help facilitate future learning about the seasons, children need to recognise how hours of daylight change through the year.

TIPS

- Ensure all children know the difference between light and dark before you begin your books.
- Tell parents you are asking children this, so they can focus on how light or dark it is at bedtime and in the mornings.

WHAT TO DO

- Give each child a book and explain that it will be finished when all four seasons have passed.
- Talk about how light it is at the three times of day you have written down.
- Ask children to colour the first window to show how light it was when they they got up and to draw themselves getting up.
- Repeat for lunch and bedtime.
- Bring the books out again in the following season and fill in the next page.
- When you have covered all four seasons, discuss and remind children what it was like to go to bed when it was dark/light etc.

6 How do you feel today?

Materials and preparation

- card circles with one of the following faces drawn on: happy, sad, worried, excited
- 4 card circles for each child
- pencil crayons or felt-tipped pens

To talk about their experiences. To use emotion words

To reflect on their own feelings. To show understanding for the feelings of others

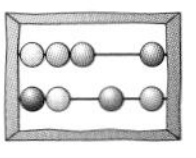

To sort, match and count

Reinforce seasonal learning by asking children to reflect how the weather affects their feelings.

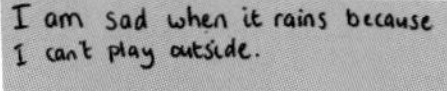

I am sad when it rains because I can't play outside.

I am happy when it rains because I like jumping in puddes.

EXTENSION IDEAS

- Base your storytime for the week on what makes us happy or sad. Start with 'Bad Mood Bear' and 'Little Bird' to cover feeling cross and sad (see resources).

Questions

- What makes you happy/sad/excited/fed up?
- What is the weather like today?
- How do you feel on sunny/rainy/windy/cold/snowy days?
- Can you show me a fed up face?

WHAT TO DO

- Talk with the children about how they are feeling today.
- Direct their attention towards the weather and discuss how they feel about different kinds.
- Ask children to make faces showing different emotions.
- Show them the card circles you have made and ask them to make their own.
- Say a kind of weather and ask each child to choose the appropriate card to match their feelings for that weather.
- Talk about their different choices e.g. the sun may worry some children if they burn.
- Let the children make pictures to show how they feel about different kinds of weather. Scribe their comments.

7 Life cycles

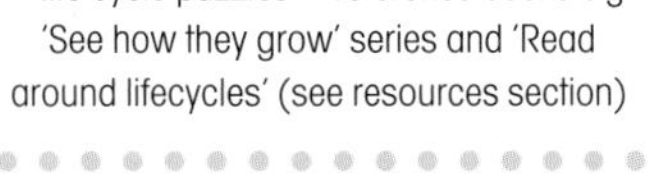

Materials and preparation

- life cycle puzzles
- reference books e.g. 'See how they grow' series and 'Read around lifecycles' (see resources section)

To show concern and care for living things. To work independently

To recognise and explore objects in the natural world. To be curious about the world around them. To ask questions to find out why things happen

TIP Carefully collect caterpillars in nets or containers to study. Try not to touch them. Keep them in clear magnifying jars with leaves from the plant on which they were found. Let children watch and draw the caterpillars. Keep the caterpillars for one session only.

Use life cycle toys and puzzles to help children work out the seasonal life cycles of creatures such as butterflies and frogs.

When drawing caterpillars, chalks or oil pastels are good for getting a 'furry' feel.

WHAT TO DO

- Choose a seasonal life cycle to explore with the children. Share the reference books with the children so that they can learn the sequence of the life cycle.
- Introduce appropriate language, such as egg, larvae, cocoon, frog spawn, tadpole and so on.
- Now give the children the relevant life cycle puzzle or game to complete. Let children work independently or in pairs to build the life cycles.
- Encourage the children to start with an egg and move forward.

Wildlife and conservation groups recommend that you do not collect frog spawn from ponds.

8 How have you changed?

Materials and preparation

- scrap book for each child made from large pieces of sugar paper stapled together
- pencils, crayons etc.
- glue

To reflect on their own learning. To initiate ideas. To be confident in their own abilities

To talk in small and large groups. To know that pictures and words convey meaning. To understand that writing serves different purposes

To talk about experiences in their own lives, both past and present

TIP Most settings keep achievement folders but these are not always available to children to look at, add to, talk about or take home. Personal year books could add this dimension to record keeping.

Making a personal My Year scrapbook can help children to reflect on their development and encourage them to continue to progress.

Make the scrap books more durable by giving them laminated card covers.

If you have access to a digital camera or scanner you could make the scrap books electronically.

WHAT TO DO

- Regularly set aside time to talk to children on a one-to-one basis about their latest achievements or interests. Ask them to record this in their books.
- Photograph the children once a term to put in their books, too.
- If significant events occur at other times, encourage children to record them in their book with e.g. a drawing or souvenir.
- Encourage parents to note important milestones or events and send in contributions as well.
- As the child's nursery year or the school or calendar year, draws to a close, look at the books again and talk about all the changes that have happened.

Musical change

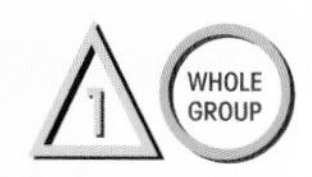

Materials and preparation

- 'Seasons' storybook (see resources)
- range of instruments e.g. chime bars, drums and tambours, shakers of all sorts, cabassas and guiros, claves and triangles, bells, finger cymbals and large cymbals if noise isn't an issue
- cassette tape recorder
- cassette tape

To make choices and decisions

To play a variety of instruments

To respond imaginatively through music

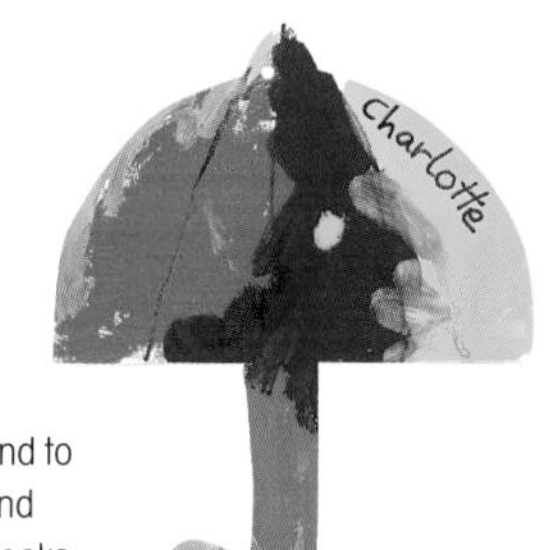

To respond to stories and picture books

WHAT TO DO

Talk with children about creating a piece of music that goes through each season in order. Write down their suggestions and decide together which of these things they would like to represent in their music. Let children suggest and try out instruments for each suggestion. Ask the group to comment constructively on whether or not the instrument and tempo is appropriate. Starting with spring, agree which sounds should be used and in what order. Practise the music until children feel confident they can remember it and allow them to suggest any improvements. Repeat for the remaining seasons and put them all together.

Share this poem with children to reinforce their learning and understanding of the seasons.

The Months

January brings snow,
Makes our feet and fingers glow.

February brings the rain,
Thaws the lakes again.

March brings breezes loud and shrill,
Stirs the dancing daffodil.

April brings the primrose sweet,
Scatters daisies at our feet.

May brings flocks of pretty lambs,
Skipping by their fleecy dams.

June brings tulips, lilies, roses,
Fills the children's hands with posies.

Hot July brings cooling showers,
Apricots and gillyflowers.

August brings the sheaves of corn,
Then the harvest home is borne.

Warm September brings the fruit,
Sportsmen then begin to shoot.

Fresh October brings the pheasant,
Then to gather nuts is pleasant.

Dull November brings the blast,
Then the leaves are whirling fast.

Chill December brings the sleet,
Blazing fire, and Christmas treat.

Sara Coleridge

WHAT TO DO

- Read the whole poem to the children and then repeat it verse by verse.
- Discuss the features of each month with the children.
- Now group the verses into seasons and share them with the children.

Make sound effects to accompany the poem. Use home-made shakers with different fillings, rustly paper, clapping and tapping with hands, fingers and feet, scraping different surfaces etc.

TIP If the children find it hard to think of things to represent each season, remind them of the poem.

- Share 'Seasons' storybook (see resources).

Resources

The resources section provides a useful range of material to supplement the activities in this book. The booklist below contains a selection of stories, information books, poems, and songs. You will find templates for some of the creative activities on pages 62-63 and the index on page 64 lists every activity contained in **All About Seasons**.

Information books

'Autumn Festivals', 'Spring Festivals', 'New Year', (Get set ... Go series) Helen Bliss. Watts

'Butterfly', S. Savage. Wayland

'Changes, Changes', Pat Hutchins. The Bodley Head

'Farm Animals', 'Baby Animals', (DK Eye Openers series) Dorling Kindersley

'My First Nature Book', Angela Wilkes. Dorling Kindersley

'Duck', 'Frog', 'Rabbit' and 'Butterfly', (I am a ... series) David Bennett Books

'Pond and River', Eyewitness Guides. Dorling Kindersley

'Puppy', 'Lamb', 'Calf', (See How They Grow series) Dorling Kindersley

'Changing Seasons', 'Flowers', 'Trees', 'The Weather', 'The Seashore', (Walkabout series) Watts Books

'My First Look at Seasons'. Dorling Kindersley

'Why Do Seasons Change?' Dorling Kindersley

Poetry books

'First Poems', Julia Eccleshare. Orchard Books

'Out and About', Shirley Hughes. Walker Books

'Poems for the Very Young', Michael Rosen, Kingfisher

'Read Aloud Rhymes for the Very Young', Jack Prelutsky. Walker Books

Story books

'A year in Percy's park', Nick Butterworth. Harper Collins

'Bad Mood Bear', John Richardson. Red Fox

'The Big Alfie Out of Doors Story Book', Shirley Hughes. Red Fox

'The Boy With Two Shadows', Margaret Mahy. Puffin Picture Books

'Changes, Changes', Pat Hutchins. Red Fox

'Kipper's Weather', Mick Inkpen. Hodder and Stoughton

'Little Bird', Rod Campbell. Campbell Books

'Once there were giants', Martin Waddell and Penny Dale. Walker Books

'Season', Siobhan Dodds. Franklin Watts

'Seasons', John Burningham. Jonathan Cape

'The Tiny Seed', Eric Carle. Hodder Children's Books

'Today is Monday', Eric Carle. Puffin Books

'When the Wind Stops', Charlotte Zolotow. Harper Collins

Resources by season

Spring

'I am a ...' series. David Bennett Books

'In the Small, Small Pond', Denise Fleming. The Bodley Head

'Mrs Mopple's Washing Line', Anita Hewett. Red Fox

'See How They Grow' series. Dorling Kindersley

'Spot goes to the farm', Eric Hill. Heinemann

'The Spring Rabbit', Joyce Dunbar and Susan Varley. Andersen Press

'The Wind Blew', Pat Hutchins. Red Fox

'Where Is My Baby?', Harriet Ziefert and Simms Tabak. Harper Collins

Summer

'Aardvark's Picnic', Jon Atlas Higham. Macmillan

'Amanda's Butterfly', Nick Butterworth. Picture Lions

'Butterfly Kiss', Vicki Churchill and Charles Fuge. Hodder Children's books

'Having a Picnic', Sarah Garland. Puffin Books

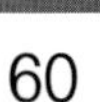

Resources

'If My Dog Went on Holiday', Bernice Lum. Bloomsbury Children's books
'It's the Bear', Jez Alborough. Walker Books
'Little Bean's Holiday', John Wallace. Collins
'The Long Weekend', Troon Harrison. Red Fox
'Lucy and Tom at the Seaside', Shirley Hughes. Victor Gollancz Ltd
'The picnic',Ruth Brown. Red Fox
'Sports Day', Nick Butterwoth and Mick Inkpen. Hodder Children's Books
'Teddy bear's Picnic', Mark Burgess. Collins Picture Lions
'The Very Hungry Caterpillar', Eric Carle. Hodder Children's Books

AUTUMN

'Pumpkin Soup', Helen Cooper. Doubleday
'Ridiculous', M. Coleman. Magi Publications (looks at hibernating animals)
'Sonny's Wonderful Wellies'. Lisa Stubbs. Picadilly Press
'Wake Up Bear', L. Dodd. Puffin Books
'You and Me, Little Bear', Martin Waddell and Barbara Firth. Walker Books

WINTER

'Buster Keeps Warm', Rod Campbell. Campbell Books
'Elmer in the Snow', David McKee. Andersen Press
'Frog in Winter', Max Velthuijs. Andersen Press
'Kipper's Snowy Day', Mick Inkpen. Hodder Children's Books
'The Last Dragon', Susan Miho Nunes. Clarion Books Houghton Mifflin
'Little Mo', Martin Waddell. Walker Books
'One Snowy Night', Nick Butterworth. Picture Lions
'Ridiculous', M. Coleman. Magi Publications (looks at winter weather)
'Ten out of bed', Penny Dale. Walker Books
'The Snow Lambs', Debi Gliori. Scholastic
'The Snowman Story Book', Raymond Briggs. Puffin

MUSIC & VIDEOS

'Four Seasons' by Vivaldi available as a cassette tape or CD from music shops
'Harlequin, 44 songs round the year'. A&C Black. Contains lots of songs about the months of the year and seasons
'Never Smile at a crocodile' cassette tape produced by The Early Learning Centre
'Sing a rainbow', Apusskidu. A&C Black
'The Snowman', Columbia/Tristar

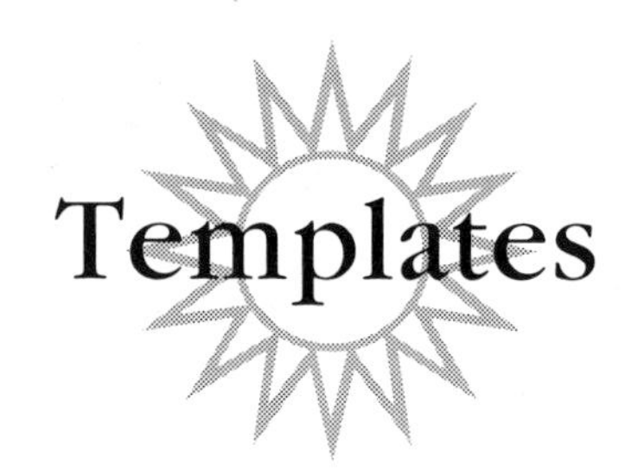

Templates

Shadow puppet templates for
Make a shadow theatre (6) page 23

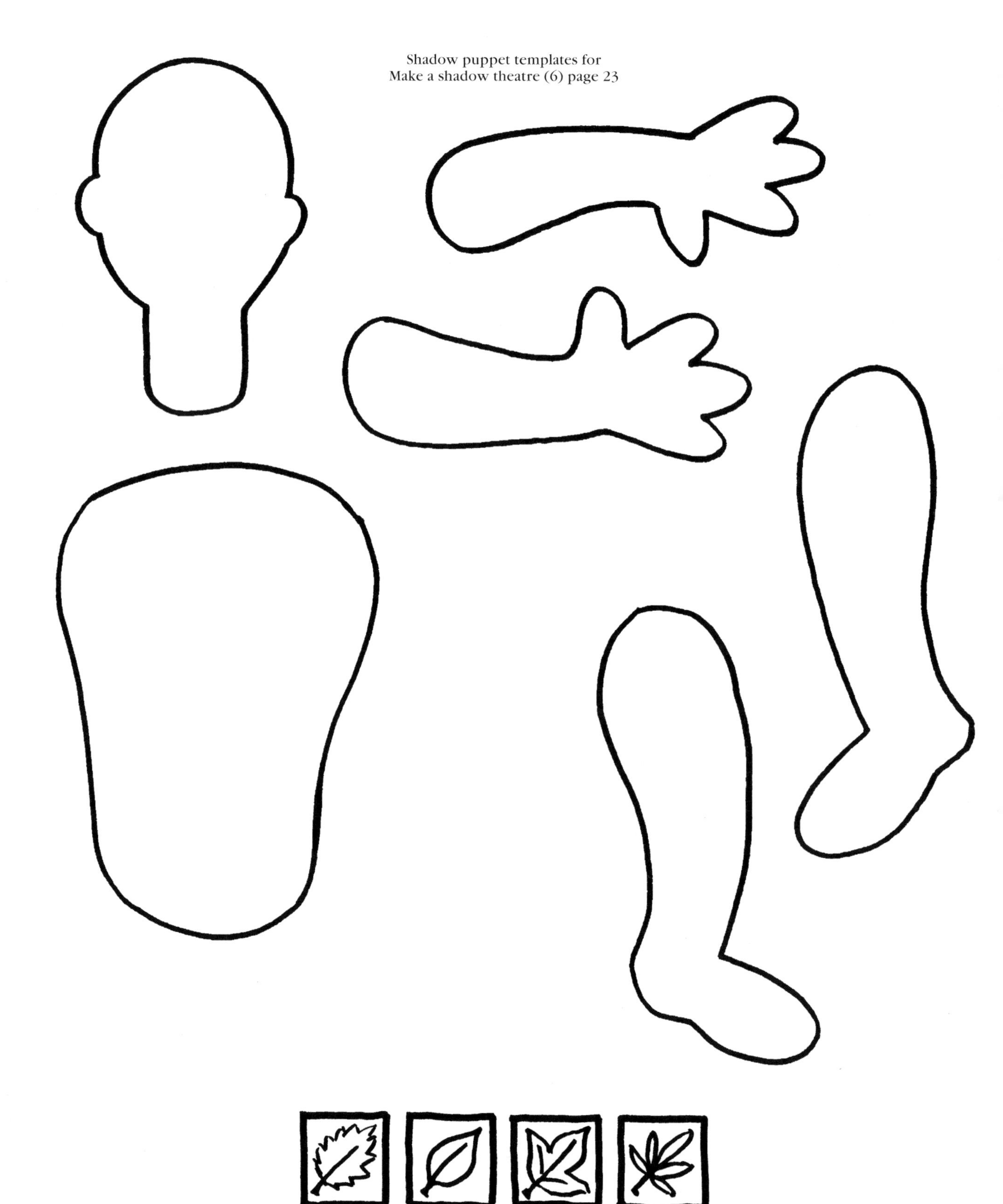

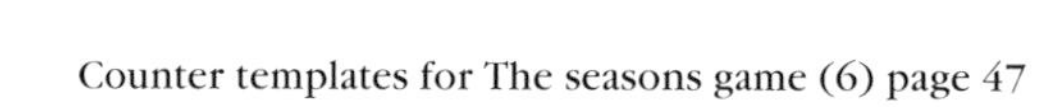

Counter templates for The seasons game (6) page 47

Base board template for The seasons game (6) page 47

Index

Acknowledgments

Nursery World would like to thank:

Hope Education for providing many of the props used in this book; Clare Shedden and Jim Copley for props and templates; Neil Thompson for digital music; Colin Bunner for digital artwork; Emma Pym for editorial assistance; Denise Blake for picture research

Lucy Tizzard for the photograph bottom centre of page 17; A-Z Botanical Ltd for the photograph top of page 56